FROM RITUAL TO THEATRE

05 04 03 02 01 00 99 98   7 6 5 4

Distributed by The Johns Hopkins University Press
2715 North Charles Street, Baltimore, Maryland 21218

Library of Congress Cataloging in Publication Data
From Ritual to Theatre: The Human Seriousness of Play
Library of Congress Catalog Card No.: 81-83751
ISBN: 0-933826-16-8 cloth
ISBN: 0-933826-17-6 paper

Printed in the United States of America on acid-free paper

A catalog record for this book is available from the British Library.

From Ritual to Theatre

The Human Seriousness of Play

Victor Turner

PAJ Publications
A Division of Performing Arts Journal, Inc.
New York

This is the first volume of the Performance Studies Series edited by Brooks McNamara and Richard Schechner. The Series is published by Performing Arts Journal Publications.

GENERAL INTRODUCTION TO THE PERFORMANCE STUDIES SERIES

What is a performance? A play? Dancers dancing? A concert? What you see on TV? Circus and Carnival? A press conference by whoever is President? The shooting of the Pope as portrayed by media—or the instant replays of Lee Harvey Oswald being shot? And do these events have anything to do with ritual, a week with Grotowski in the woods outside of Wroclaw, or a Topeng masked dance drama as performed in Peliatan, Bali? Performance is no longer easy to define or locate: the concept and structure has spread all over the place. It is ethnic and intercultural, historical and ahistorical, aesthetic and ritual, sociological and political. Performance is a mode of behavior, an approach to experience; it is play, sport, aesthetics, popular entertainments, experimental theatre, and more. But in order for this broad perspective to develop performance must be written about with precision and in full detail. The editors of this series have designed it as a forum for investigating what performance is, how it works, and what its place in post-modern society may be. Performance Studies is not properly theatrical, cinematic, anthropological, historical, or artistic—though any of the monographs in the Series incorporate one or more of these disciplines. Because we are fostering a new approach to the study of performance, we have kept the Series open-ended in order to incorporate new work. The Series, we hope, will measure the depth and breadth of the field—and its fertility: from circus to Mabou Mines, rodeo to healing rites, Black performance in South Africa to the Union City Passion Play. Performance Studies will be valuable for scholars in all areas of performance as well as for theatre workers who want to expand and deepen their notions of performance.

Brooks McNamara
Richard Schechner

Contents

Introduction

The essays in this book chart my personal voyage of discovery from traditional anthropological studies of ritual performance to a lively interest in modern theatre, particularly experimental theatre. In a way, though, the trip was also a "return of the repressed," for my mother, Violet Witter, had been a founding member and actress in the Scottish National Theater, located in Glasgow, which aimed, in the 1920s, at being the equivalent of, if not the answer to, the great Dublin Abbey Theater. Alas, Scots Celts, tainted by Norman and Calvinist forebears, could not emulate the heady nationalist eloquence or stark political metacommentary of an Ireland struggling to be free, an Ireland rich in bards and playwrights. The National Theater soon folded. But my mother remained a woman of the theatre to the end, and, Ruth Draper-like, would give solo performances, drawing her repertoire from such (then) rebel voices as Ibsen, Shaw, Strindberg, O'Casey, Olive Schreiner, and Robert Burns ("A Man's a Man for a' That"). She was also something of a feminist and included in her stock of roles a selection entitled "Great Women from Great Plays," which ranged from Euripides, through Shakespeare and Webster, Congreve and Wycherly, to such an odd bunch of "moderns" as James Barrie, Fiona McLeod (actually the critic William Sharp in literary Celtic "drag"), Clemence Dane (Queen Elizabeth in "Will Shakespeare"), and Shaw once again ("Great Catherine" and "Candida"). The recurrent theme was female charisma, the sort of willed or innate queenliness that cowed would-be dominant males. My father, though, was an electrical (in American terms, "electronic") engineer, an inventive businessman who had worked intensively with John Logan Baird, a pioneer in the development of television. He had little interest or insight into theatre, though he adored the novels of H. G. Wells (particularly his science fiction), whom he had once met. Inevitably, in those C. P. Snow days of the "two cultures," that even more than Kipling's "East and West," could "never meet," they divorced, and stranded me, a fervent Scots nationalist, though only eleven years old, with retired maternal grandparents in the deep south of England, Bournemouth. Although this seaside haunt had been graced intermittently by Verlaine and Rimbaud, Walter Scott, Tolstoy, Robert Louis Stevenson, James Elroy Flecker, and other authors of less note, its nature, not its culture, moved me, its seascapes and headlands, its proximity to the New Forest, its aromatic pine trees. Separated effectively from both my parents (my mother moved around Southern England, teaching Delsarte principles and elocution to young ladies in sundry "Free Schools," while my father, still in Scotland, "went broke" in the "Thirties" slump), I slithered between arts and sciences, sports and classics. I won a prize for a poem on "Salamis" at age twelve, which excited the derision of my schoolmates for many years and forced me to win attention as a soccer player and cricketer of some violence—I shamefully acquired the proud title of "Tank"—to erase the stigma of sensibility.

No wonder, then, that in time I became an anthropologist, a member of a discipline poised uneasily between those who promote the "science of culture," on the model of the nineteenth century natural sciences, and those who show how "we" (Westerners) may share in the humanity of others (non-Westerners). The former speak in terms of monointentional materialism, the latter of mutual communication. Both approaches are probably necessary. We should try to find out how and why different sets of human beings in time and space are similar and different in their cultural manifestations; we should also explore why and how all men and women, if they work at it, can understand one another. At first I was taught by British "structural-functionalists," descendants not only of the British empiricist philosophers, Locke and Hume, but of the French positivists, Comte and Durkheim. Armchair Marxists have accused those of us who lived close to the "people" in the 1950s in African, Malaysian, and Oceanian villages, often for several years, of "using" structural functionalism to provide the "scientific" objectification of an unquestioned ideology (colonialism in prewar anthropology, neoimperialism now). These dour modern "Roundheads"—an infra-red band on the world's spectrum of Moral Majorities—have become so obsessed with power that they fail to sense the many-leveled complexity (hence irony and forgivability) of human lives experienced at first hand.

My training for fieldwork roused the scientist in me—the paternal heritage. My field experience revitalized the maternal gift of theatre. I compromised by inventing a unit of description and analysis which I called "social drama." In the field my family and I lived in no "ivory tower": we spent nearly three years in African villages (Ndembu, Lamba, Kosa, Gisu), mostly in grass huts. Something like "drama" was constantly emerging, even erupting, from the otherwise fairly even surfaces of social life. For the scientist in me, such social dramas revealed the "taxonomic" relations among actors (their kinship ties, structural positions, social class, political status, and so forth), and their contemporary bonds and oppositions of interest and friendship, their personal network ties, and informal relationships. For the artist in me, the drama revealed individual character, personal style, rhetorical skill, moral and aesthetic differences, and choices proffered and made. Most importantly, it made me aware of the power of symbols in human communication. This power inheres not only in the shared lexicons and grammars of spoken and written languages, but also in the artful or poetic individual crafting of speech through persuasive tropes: metaphors, metonyms, oxymora, "wise words" (a Western Apache speech-mode), and many more. Nor is communication through symbols limited to words. Each culture, each person within it, uses the entire sensory repertoire to convey messages: manual gesticulations, facial expressions, bodily postures, rapid, heavy, or light breathing, tears, at the individual level; stylized gestures, dance patterns, prescribed silences, synchronized movements such as marching, the moves and "plays" of games, sports, and rituals, at the cultural level. Claude Levi-Strauss was one of the first to call our attention to the diverse "sensory codes" through which information may be transmitted, and how they may be combined and mutually "translated."

Perhaps if I had not had early exposure to theatre—my first clear memory of a performance was Sir Frank Benson's version of *The Tempest* when I was five years old—I would not have been alerted to the "theatrical" potential of social life, especially in such coherent communities as African villages. But no one could fail to note the analogy, indeed the homology, between those sequences of supposedly "spontaneous" events which made fully evident the tensions existing in those villages, and the characteristic "processual form" of Western drama, from Aristotle onwards, or Western epic and saga, albeit on a limited or miniature scale. No one could fail to recognize, moreover, when "dramatic time" has replaced routinized social living. Behavior took on the character known to neurobiologists as "ergotropic." In their terms it exhibited "arousal, heightened activity, and emotional response." No doubt, had I possessed the technical means of measurement, I would have been able to discover in the "actors," such "augmented sympathetic discharges" as "increased heart rate, blood pressure, sweat secretion, pupillary dilation, and the inhibition of gastro-intestinal motor and secretory function." (Barbara Lex, "Neurobiology of Ritual Trance," in *The Spectrum of Ritual,* 1979:136). In other words, during social dramas, a group's emotional climate is full of thunder and lightning and choppy air currents! What has happened is that a public breach has occurred in the normal working of society, ranging from some grave transgression of the code of manners to an act of violence, a beating, even a homicide. Such a breach may result from real feeling, a crime passionel perhaps, or from cool calculation—a political act designed to challenge the extant power structure. Again, the breach may take the form of unhappy chance: a quarrel round the beer pots, an unwise or overheard word, an unpremeditated quarrel. Nevertheless, once antagonisms are out in the open, members of a group inevitably take sides. Or else they seek to bring about a reconciliation among the contestants. Thus *breach* slides into *crisis*, and the critics of crisis seek to restore peace. Such critics are usually those with a strong interest in maintaining the *status quo ante*, the elders, lawmakers, administrators, judges, priests, and law enforcers of the relevant community. All or some of these attempt to apply *redressive machinery*—to "patch up"quarrels, "mend" broken social ties, "seal up punctures" in the "social fabric," by the juridical means of courts and the judicial process or the ritual means provided by religious institutions: divination into the hidden causes of social conflict (witchcraft, ancestral wrath, the gods' displeasure), prophylactic sacrifice, therapeutic ritual (involving the exorcism of malefic spirits and the propitiation of "good" ones), and finding the apt occasion for the performance of a major ritual celebrating the values, common interests, and moral order of the widest recognized cultural and moral community, transcending the divisions of the local group. The social drama concludes—if ever it may be said to have a "last act"—either in the reconciliation of the contending parties or their agreement to differ—which may involve a dissident minority in seceding from the original community and seeking a new habitat (the Exodus theme, but also exemplified on a smaller scale by the splitting of Central African villages).

In large-scale modern societies, social dramas may escalate from the local level to national revolutions, or from the very beginning may take the form of war between nations. In all cases, from the familial and village level to international conflict, social dramas reveal "subcutaneous" levels of the social structure, for every "social system," from tribe to nation, to fields of international relations, is composed of many "groups," "social categories," statuses and roles, arranged in hierarchies and divided into segments. In small-scale societies there are oppositions among clans, sub-clans, lineages, families, age-sets, religious and political associations, and many more. In our own industrial societies, we are familiar with opposi-tions between classes, sub-classes, ethnic groups, sects and cults, regions, political parties, and associatons based on gender, division of labor, and relative age. Other societies are internally divided by caste and traditional craft. Social dramas have a habit of activating these "classificatory" *opposi-tions* and many more: *factions* (which may cut across traditional caste, class, or lineage *divisions* in pursuit of immediate, contemporary interests), *religious "revitalization" movements* which may mobilize former "tribal" enemies in joint opposition to foreign, colonizing overlords with superior military technology, international *alliances* and *coalitions* of ideologically disparate groups who see themselves as having a common enemy (often equally heterogeneous in national, religious, class, ideological, economic make-up), and common immediate interests—and turning them into *con-flicts*.

Social life, then, even its apparently quietest moments, is characteristically "pregnant" with social dramas. It is as though each of us has a "peace" face and a "war" face, that we are programmed for co-operation, but prepared for conflict. The primordial and perennial agonistic mode is the social drama. But as our species has moved through time and become more dexterous in the use and manipulation of symbols, as our technological mastery of nature and our powers of self-destruction have grown exponentially in the past few thousand years, in similar measure we have become somewhat more adept in devising cultural modes of confronting, understanding, assigning meaning to, ·and sometimes cop-ing with crisis—the second stage of the ineradicable social drama that besets us at all times, all places, and all levels of sociocultural organization. The third stage, modes of redress, which always contained at least the germ of self-reflexivity, a public way of assessing our social behavior, has moved out of the domains of law and religion into those of the various arts. The growing complexity of the social and economic division of labor, giving specialization and professionalization their opportunity to escape from embedment in the total ongoing social process, has also provided complex sociocultural systems with effective instruments for scrutinizing themselves. By means of such genres as theatre, including puppetry and shadow theatre, dance drama, and professional story-telling, performances are presented which probe a community's weaknesses, call its leaders to ac-count, desacralize its most cherished values and beliefs, portray its characteristic conflicts and suggest remedies for them, and generally take stock of its current situation in the known "world."

Thus the roots of theatre are in social drama, and social drama accords well with Aristotle's abstraction of dramatic form from the works of the

Greek playwrights. But theatre in complex, urbanized societies on the scale of "civilizations" has become a specialized domain, where it has become legitimate to experiment with modes of presentation, many of which depart radically (and, indeed, consciously) from Aristotle's model. But these sophisticated departures are themselves implicit in the fact that theatre owes its specific genesis to the third phase of social drama, a phase which is essentially an attempt to ascribe meaning to "social dramatic" events by the process which Richard Schechner has recently described as "restoring the past." Theatre is, indeed, a hypertrophy, an exaggeration, of jural and ritual processes; it is not a simple replication of the "natural" total processual pattern of the social drama. There is, therefore, in theatre something of the investigative, judgmental, and even punitive character of law-in-action, and something of the sacred, mythic, numinous, even "supernatural" character of religious action—sometimes to the point of sacrifice. Grotowski hit off this aspect well with his terms, "holy actor," and "secular sacrum."

The positivist and functionalist schools of anthropology in whose concepts and methods I was first instructed could give me only limited insight into the dynamics of social dramas. I could count the people involved, state their social status-roles, describe their behavior, collect biographical information about them from others, and place them structurally in the social system of the community manifested by the social drama. But this way of treating "social facts as things," as the French sociologist Durkheim admonished investigators to do, gave little understanding of the motives and characters of the actors in these purpose-saturated, emotional, and "meaningful" events. I gradually gravitated, with temporary pauses to study symbolic processes, theories of symbolic interaction, the views of sociological phenomenologists, and those of French structuralists and "deconstructionists," towards the basic stance delineated by the great German social thinker, whose photographs remind one of a grizzled old peasant, Wilhelm Dilthey (1833-1911). This stance depends upon the concept of experience (in German, *Erlebnis,* literally "what has been *lived* through"). Kant had argued that the data of experience are "formless." Dilthey disagreed. He conceded that any distinguishable "manifold," whether a natural formation or organism, or a cultural institution, or a mental event, contains certain formal relationships which can be analyzed. Dilthey called these the "formal categories": unity and multiplicity, likeness and difference, whole and part, degree, and similar elementary concepts. As H. A. Hodges, writing on Dilthey (1953:68-9) summarized: "All the forms of discursive thought, as analyzed in formal logic, and all the fundamental concepts of mathematics, can be reduced to these formal categories. They are a network within which all thought about any subject-matter must be enclosed. They are applicable to all possible objects of thought, *but they express the peculiar nature of none of them* (my emphasis); and, as without them nothing can be understood, *so nothing can be understood with them alone*" (my emphasis).

Dilthey goes on to argue that experience, in its formal aspect, is richer than can be accounted for by general formal categories. It is not that the experiencing subject *imposes* such categories as space, substance, causal interaction, and so forth on the physical world, or duration, creative freedom, value, significance, and the like on the "world of mind." Rather, the data of experience are "instinct with form," and thought's work is to draw out "the structural system" implicit in every distinguishable *Erlebnis* or unit of experience, whether this be a love affair or a historical cause célèbre such as the Dreyfus Affair—or a social drama.

Structures of experience, for Dilthey, are not the bloodless "cognitive structures," static and "synchronic," so beloved of the "thought-structuralists" who have dominated French anthropology for so long. Cognition is, of course, an important aspect, facet, or "dimension" of any structure of experience. Thought clarifies and generalizes lived experience, but experience is charged with emotion and volition, sources respectively of value-judgments and precepts. Behind Dilthey's world-picture is the basic fact of the total human being (Lawrence's "man alive") at grips with his environment, perceiving, thinking, feeling, desiring. As he says, "life embraces life." As Hodges continues: "All the intellectual and linguistic structures which philosophers study, and from whose complexities and obscurities the problems of philosophy arise are incidents in this interaction between man and his world" (*op. cit.*, p. 349).

For me, the anthropology of performance is an essential part of the anthropology of experience. In a sense, every type of cultural performance, including ritual, ceremony, carnival, theatre, and poetry, is explanation and explication of life itself, as Dilthey often argued. Through the performance process itself, what is normally sealed up, inaccessible to everyday observation and reasoning, in the depth of sociocultural life, is drawn forth — Dilthey uses the term *Ausdruck*, "an expression," from *ausdrucken*, literally, "to press or squeeze out." "Meaning" is squeezed out of an event which has either been directly experienced by the dramatist or poet, or cries out for penetrative, imaginative understanding (*Verstehen*). An experience is itself a process which "presses out" to an "expression" which completes it. Here the etymology of "performance" may give us a helpful clue, for it has nothing to do with "form," but derives from Old French *parfournir*, "to complete" or "carry out thoroughly." A performance, then, is the proper finale of an experience. Dilthey's presentation of the five "moments" of *Erlebnis* have a processual structure, being genetically connected. Each *Erlebnis* or distinctive experience has (1) a perceptual core —pleasure or pain may be felt more intensely than in routinized, repetitive behaviors; (2) images of past experiences are evoked with "unusual clarity of outline, strength of sense, and energy of projection" (cited in R.A. Makreel, 1975:141). (3) But past events remain inert unless the feelings originally bound up with them can be fully revived; (4) "meaning" is generated by "feelingly" thinking about the interconnections between past and present events. Here Dilthey distinguishes between "meaning" (*Bedeutung*) and value (*Wert*). Value belongs essentially to an experience in a conscious present. Value inheres in the affective enjoyment of the present. Values are not inwardly connected with one another in a systematic way. As Dilthey put it: "From the standpoint of value, life appears as an infinite assortment of positive and negative existence-values. It is like a chaos of harmonies and discords. Each of these is a tone-structure which fills a present; but they have no musical relation to one another." But it is in bringing past and present into "musical relation" that the process of discovering and establishing "meaning" consists. But it is not enough to possess a meaning for oneself; (5) an experience is never truly completed until it is "expressed," that is, until it is communicated in terms intelligible to others, linguistic or otherwise. Culture itself is the ensemble of such expressions—the experience of individuals made available to society and accessible to the sympathetic penetration of other "minds." For this reason Dilthey thought of culture as "objectified mind" (*objectiver Geist*). According to Dilthey, "our knowledge of what is given in experience is extended through the interpretation of the objectifications of life and this interpretation, in turn, is only made possible by plumbing the depths of subjective experience" (*Dilthey: Selected Writings*, 1976:195-6). Thus, we can know our own subjective depths as much by scrutinizing the meaningful objectifications "expressed" by other minds, as by introspection. In complementary fashion, self-scrutiny may give us clues to the penetration of objectifications of life generated from the experience of others. There is a kind of "hermeneutic circle" involved here, or rather, "spiral," for each turn transcends its predecessor.

Expressions, for Dilthey, may be of several classes. There are "ideas," which can be transmitted precisely, since they have a high degree of generality. But they tell us nothing about the particular person's consciousness in which they first appeared. "Our understanding here is precise, but it is not deep," says Dilthey (*op. cit.*, G.S., VII, 205-6). "It tells us what idea someone has, but not how he comes to have it" (*ibid.*). A second class of expression is that of human "acts." Every act, Dilthey argues, is the execution of a purpose, a volition, and, since the relation between act and purpose is regular and intimate, the purpose can be read in the act. The act was done not to express the purpose, but to fulfil it; nevertheless to an outside observer, it does in fact express what it fulfils (Hodges, *op. cit.*, p. 130). This applies not only to the acts of an agent's private life, but also to the public acts of legislators, and the behavior of masses of people in public situations. In describing and analyzing social dramas in Africa and elsewhere, for instance, I have become very much aware of the relationship between acts and purposes and goals, though I would go further than Dilthey and see many acts as expressing and fulfilling *unconscious purposes and goals.*

This unconscious formative component is even more important where the third class of expressions—works of art—is concerned. Dilthey must have been aware of its importance when he wrote (*Gesammelte Schriften,* henceforth cited as "G.S.," Vol. VII, 1927:206): "I set before myself the sum of Goethe's artistic, literary, and scientific publications, and the rest of his writings. . . . Here the problem can be solved of understanding the inner reality, *in a certain sense better than* Goethe understood himself." Works of art are vastly unlike many expressions of political experience, which lie under the power of selfish or partisan interests, and hence suppress, distort, or counterfeit the products of authentic experience. Artists have no motive for deceit or concealment, but strive to find the perfect expressive form for their experience. As Wilfred Owen wrote: "The true poets must be truthful." In some way they have an innocent prehension of that strange liminal space—in all of us, but more speakingly so in artists—where, as Dilthey writes, "life discloses itself at a depth inaccessible to observation, reflection, and theory" (Vol. VII, 1927:207). Once "expressed," however, as works of art, readers, viewers, and hearers can reflect upon them since they are trustworthy messages from our species' depths, humanized life disclosing itself, so to speak.

Recapitulating, then, we have traced a path from the third phase of social drama to theatrical performance, which is then connected with the "fifth moment" of a Diltheyan *Erlebnis,* or as structured unit of experience. It is in this moment that the poet, artist, or dramatist "freely unfolds images beyond the bounds of reality" (Dilthey, G.S., VI, 1924:137). The artist tries to penetrate the very essence of the *Erlebnis.* In so doing he allows free access to the depths where "life grasps life."

In the past five years, I have been directly introduced by Richard Schechner to the workings of the experimental theatre which flourished in the United States in the late 1960s and early 1970s, but appears regrettably to be merely sputtering today. Several of the essays in this book relate to Schechner's theories and practice as a producer. Schechner's theatre was alive to the social dramas of our time, and sought "by freely unfolding images beyond the bounds of reality" to lay hold of the nature of its predicament. Indeed, the entire process which he set in train after deciding upon a dramatic theme was almost a transformation into overt, public terms of Dilthey's inner movement from *Erlebnis* as direct experience to its meaningful, aesthetic outcome as a work of art. "Direct experience" was usually some problem in Schechner's own life or in that of the Performance Group, of which he was director. He then set about finding a "text" or "script" which would give him a mirror, serve as a reflexive device, for scrutinizing his problem. "Direct experience" was also involved in the casting process, whose complexities I have no room to discuss here. Next began the "Workshop" process, which often lasted for over a year, and which I once likened to the forest camp where novices are initiated in African circumcision rituals, dedicated to the imparting of esoteric knowledge, training in useful, practical techniques, subjecting the neophytes to ordeals, confronting them with masked, numinous figures representing remote tribal ancestors and deities, portraying origin myths, and, in effect, dissolving their former social personalities in order to "regrow" them, to use a widely known African expression, as self-disciplined, mature persons. As is customary in "postmodern" (i.e., post-World War II) theatre, the text is sometimes composed—or playwrights' texts are decomposed, then recomposed—during rehearsals. Texts are not privileged. Theatrical space, performers, director, media used (amplification and distortion of speech, television screens, films, slides, tapes, music, lip-synch performing, fireworks, and many more), sustained separation of role and performer by many devices, all such units and devices are flexibly combined and recombined as reflections of a common will arising from rare moments of communitas among the human components of the theatric ensemble.

These multiple and indeterminate means and codes are tentative and experimental responses to the *experience* of members of the postmodern theatre subculture as members of the new biosphere-noosphere (in Teilhardian terms) created by the qualitative leap in global communications and transportation, the computerization of myriad "bits" of information, the tentacular spread of multinational corporations headed by invisible oligarchies who eschew direct political recognition, and above all the Damoclessword of nuclear destruction which objectively threatens all and subjectively halts humanistic, "modern" progressivism in mid-stride. Schechner makes this point in a recent article, "The End of Humanism" in *Performing Arts Journal,* 10/11. However, in this article, he equates "experience" with "ordinary happenings along a linear plane," "narrative" (p. 11) and "the meaningful" (p. 13) and consigns it to the now surpassed "modern," essentially Renaissance view of human action. But the term cannot be circumscribed so narrowly in space and time. "Experience" is a word which has survived, in many cognate forms, in many languages derived from Proto-Indo-European. By analogy with geology, archaeology, and depth psychology, it may be possible to regard the etymology of key terms in major languages as a many-leveled system whose strata are composed of successively deposited layers of historical "experience." Etymology is, after all, a mode of "restoring the past," a form of linguistic "self-reflexivity." The many-leveled or "laminated" geological crust of the earth is still "alive" (think of the Mt. St. Helen's eruption); even more so is the human "mind" or "psyche," with its conscious, pre-conscious, and unconscious levels, each subdivided into layers or bands laid down by repeated dramatic or "traumatic experiences." Neurobiologists of the central nervous system recognize surviving "archaic" structures in the brain, forebrain, and autonomic systems, which continue to interact with the neocortex. Similarly, a modern word's past "senses" have influenced its present penumbra of meaning.

Scholars, such as Julius Pokorny (*Indogermanisches Etymolgisches Worterbuch*, 1959), trace "experience" right back to hypothetical Indo-European base or root *per-, "to attempt, venture, risk," whence the Greek *peira*, "experience," the source of our word "empirical." It is also the verbal root from which derives the Germanic *feraz, giving rise to Old English *faer*, "danger, sudden calamity," whence Modern English "fear." Already, then we see "cognitive" directions taken by *per-, through the Greek route, and affective ones, through the Germanic—which would have interested Dilthey, one may be sure! But more directly "experience" derives, *via* Middle English and Old French, from the Latin *experientia*, denoting "trial, proof, experiment," itself generated from *experiens*, the present participle of *experiri*, "to try, test," from *ex-*, "out" + base *per* as in *peritus*, "experienced," "having learned by trying." The suffixed extended form of *per- is *peri-tlo, whence the Latin *periclum, periculum*, "trial, danger, peril." Once more, we find experience linked with risk, straining towards "drama," crisis, rather than bland cognitive learning! The·suffixed form of I. E. *per-, *per-ya, emerges in the Greek *peira*, as mentioned, but what failed to be mentioned is that the English "pirate" comes from that Greek word, *via* *peirates*, an "attacker," from *peiran*, "to attempt, attack." Going further back, etymologists, such as Walter Skeat and Pokorny, hold that the verbal root *per- is part of a phonetically similar group, whose central concept is perhaps the base of prepositions and preverbs with the core meaning of "forward," "through." Thus the Greek verb *perao*, means "I pass *through.*" If cultural institutions and symbolic modes are to be seen, in Diltheyan terms, as the crystallized secretions of once living human experience, individual and collective, we may perhaps see the word "experience" itself as an experienced traveler through time! Or we may metaphorize it as "tree," whose tap-root is the idea of "perilous passage," even "rites of passage." From *per-, too, derive our words "fare" and "ferry"—by Grimm's Law describing the regular changes undergone by Indo-European stop consonants (in this case, *p* to *f*) represented in Germanic. Finally, "experiment," like "experience," is derived from Latin *experiri*, "to try or test." If we put these various senses together we have a "laminated" semantic system focused on "experience," which portrays it as a journey, a test (of self, of suppositions about others), a ritual passage, an exposure to peril or risk, a source of fear. By means of experience, we "fare" "fearfully" through "perils," taking "experimental" steps. It all sounds rather like Dilthey's description of *erleben*, "living through" a sequence of events—it may be a ritual, a pilgrimage, a social drama, a friend's death, a protracted labor, and other *Erlebnisse*. Such an experience is incomplete, though, unless one of its "moments" is "performance," an act of creative retrospection in which "meaning" is ascribed to the events and parts of experience—even if the meaning is that "there is no meaning." Thus experience is both "living through" and "thinking back." It is also "willing or wishing forward," i.e., establishing goals and models for future experience in which, hopefully, the errors and perils of past experience will be avoided or eliminated.

"Experimental" theatre is nothing less than "performed," in other words, "restored" experience, that moment in the experiental process—that often prolonged and internally segmented "moment"—in which meaning emerges through "reliving" the original experience (often a social drama subjectively perceived), and is given an appropriate aesthetic form. This form then becomes a piece of communicable wisdom, assisting others (through *Verstehen*, understanding) to understand better not only themselves but also the times and cultural conditions which compose their general "experience" of reality. Both Richard Schechner and I, approaching the issue from different directions, envision theatre as an important means for the intercultural transmission of painfully achieved modalities of experience. Perfect transcultural understanding may never be achieved, but if we enact one another's social dramas, rituals, and theatrical performances in full awareness of the salient characteristics of their original sociocultural settings, the very length and intensity of what Schechner calls "the training-rehearsal-preparation process" must draw the actors into "other ways of seeing" and apprehending the "reality" our symbolic formations are forever striving to encompass and express.

I began this introduction on a autobiographical note and end it with an appeal for global cultural understanding. In Charlottesville, Virginia, where I now teach at the university, the phrase "Mr. Jefferson would have approved of that," is the final seal of approval for any action. I imagine correlatively that "Professor Dilthey would have approved" of attempts being made by a handful of anthropologists and theatre scholars and practitioners to generate an anthropology and theatre of experience which seek to "understand other people and their expressions on the basis of experience and self-understanding and the constant interaction between them" (*Dilthey: Selected Writings*, 1976:218). Here the "other people" include those of every culture and every land for whom we have rich enough records to draw on for performative purposes. The ethnographies, literatures, ritual, and theatrical traditions of the world now lie open to us as the basis for a new transcultural communicative synthesis through performance. For the first time we may be moving towards a sharing of cultural experiences, the manifold "forms of objectivated mind" restored through performance to something like their pristine affectual contouring. This may be a humble step for mankind away from the destruction that surely awaits our species if we continue to cultivate deliberate mutual misunderstanding in the interests of power and profit. We *can* learn from experience—from the enactment and performance of the culturally transmitted experiences of others—peoples of the Heath as well as of the Book.

References

Dilthey, Wilhelm. *Gesammelte Schriften*. Stuttgart: Teubner; Gottingen: Vandenhoeck & Ruprecht. Vol. VI, 1924; vol. VII, 1927.

—. *Selected Writings*. Ed. and introduced by H.P. Rickman, London: Cambridge University Press (1st published 1883-1911), 1976.

Hodges, H.A. *The Philosophy of Wilhelm Dilthey*. London: Routledge and Kegan Paul, 1953.

Lex, Barbara. "Neurobiology of Ritual Trance" in *The Spectrum of Ritual*. Eds. E. d'Aquili, C. Laughlin, Jr., and J. McManus, New York: Columbia University Press, pp. 117-151, 1979.

Makreel, Rudolf A. *Dilthey: Philosopher of the Human Studies*. Princeton: Princeton University Press, 1975.

Pokorny, Julius. *Indogermanisches Etymolgisches Worterbuch*. Bern, 1959.

Schechner, Richard. "The End of Humanism," *Performing Arts Journal, 10/11, vol. IV, nos. 1-2, 1979.*

Liminal to Liminoid, in Play, Flow, and Ritual

An Essay in Comparative Symbology

First I will describe what I mean by "'comparative symbology" and how, in a broad way, it differs from such disciplines as "semiotics" (or "semiology") and "symbolic anthropology," which are also concerned with the study of such terms as symbols, signs, signals, significations, indexes, icons, signifiers, signifieds, sign-vehicles, denotata, etc. I want rather to discuss some of the types of socio-cultural processes and settings in which new symbols, verbal and non-verbal, tend to be generated. This will lead me into a comparison of "liminal' and "liminoid" phenomena, terms which I will consider shortly.

According to Webster's New World Dictionary, "symbology" is "the study or interpretation of symbols"; it is also "representation or expression by means of symbols." The term "comparative" merely means that this branch of study involves comparison as a method, as does, for example, comparative linguistics. Comparative symbology is narrower than "semiotics" or "semiology" (to use Saussure's and Roland Barthes's term), and wider than "symbolic anthropology" in range and scope of data and problems. "Semiotics" is, as everyone knows, "a general theory of signs and symbols, especially the analysis of the nature and relationship of signs in language, usually including three branches: syntactics, semantics, and pragmatics.''

(1) *Syntactics*: The formal relationships of signs and symbols to one another apart from their users or external reference; the organization and relationship of groups, phrases, clauses, sentences, and sentence structure.

(2) *Semantics*: The relationship of signs and symbols to the things to which they refer, that is, their referential meaning.

(3) *Pragmatics*: The relations of signs and symbols with their users.

In my own analysis of ritual symbols, ''syntactics'' is roughly similar to what I call ''positional meaning''; ''semantics'' is similar to ''exegetical meaning''; and ''pragmatics'' is similar to ''operational meaning.'' Semiology seems to have rather wider aspirations than semiotics, since it is defined as the ''the science of signs in general'' whereas semiotics restricts itself to signs in language, though Roland Barthes is now taking the position that ''linguistics is not a part of the general science of signs . . . it is semiology which is a part of linguistics'' (*Elements of Semiology*, p. 11).

Comparative symbology is not directly concerned with the *technical* aspects of linguistics, and has much to do with many kinds of non-verbal symbols in ritual and art, though admittedly all cultural languages have important linguistic components, relays, or ''signifieds.'' Nevertheless, it *is* involved in the relationships between symbols and the concepts, feelings, values, notions, etc. associated with them by users, interpreters or exegetes: in short it has *semantic* dimensions, it pertains to meaning in language and context. Its data are mainly drawn from *cultural genres* or *subsystems* of expressive culture. These include both oral and literate genres, and one may reckon among them *activities* combining verbal and nonverbal symbolic actions, such as ritual and drama, as well as *narrative* genres, such as myth, epic, ballad, the novel, and ideological systems. They would also include non-verbal forms, such as miming, sculpture, painting, music, ballet, and architecture. And many more.

But comparative symbology does more than merely investigate cultural genres in abstraction from human social activity. It would become semiology if it did, whose corpus of data ''must eliminate diachronic elements to the utmost'' and coincide with a ''state of the system, a cross-section of history'' (Barthes, 1967:98). In 1958 (*Forest of Symbols*, p. 20), when considering ritual data collected during my fieldwork among the Ndembu people of north-western Zambia, I wrote that ''I could not analyze [these] ritual symbols without studying them in a time series in relation to other 'events' [regarding the symbol, too, as an 'event,' rather than a 'thing'], for symbols are essentially involved in social processes [and, I would now add, in psychological processes, too]. I came to see performances of ritual as distinct phases in the social processes whereby groups became adjusted to internal changes (whether brought about by personal or factional dissensions and conflicts of norms or by technical or organizational innovations), and adapted to their external environment (social and cultural, as well as physical and biotic). From this standpoint the ritual symbol becomes a factor in social action, a positive force in an activity field. Symbols, too, are crucially involved in situations of societal change—the symbol becomes associated with human interests, purposes, ends and means, aspirations and ideals, individual and collective, whether these are explicitly formulated or have to be inferred from the observed behavior. For these reasons, the structure and properties of a ritual symbol become those of a dynamic entity, at least within its appropriate context of action.'' We shall take a closer look at some of these ''properties'' later. But I want to stress here that because *from the very outset* I formulate symbols as social and cultural dynamic systems, shedding and gathering meaning over time and altering in form, I cannot regard them merely as ''terms'' in atemporal logical or protological cognitive systems. Undoubtedly, in the specialized genres of complex societies such as philosophical, theological, and formal logical systems, symbols, and the signs derived from their decomposition, do acquire this ''algebraic'' or logical quality, and can be effectively treated in relations of ''binary opposition,'' as ''mediators,'' and the rest, denatured by the primacy of specialist cognitive activity. But ''les symboles sauvages,'' as they appear not only in traditional, ''tribal'' cultures but also in the ''cultural refreshment'' genres, of poetry, drama, and painting, of post-industrial society, have the character of dynamic semantic systems, gaining and losing meanings—and meaning in a social context always has emotional and volitional dimensions—as they ''travel through'' a *single* rite or work of art, let alone through centuries of performance, and are aimed at producing effects on the psychological states and behavior of those exposed to them or obliged to use them for their communication with other human beings. I have always tried to link my work in processual analysis, for example, studies of the ongoing process of village politics in *Schism and Continuity*, with my work in the analysis of ritual performances.

This is perhaps why I have often focused on the study of *individual* symbols, on their semantic fields and processual fate as they move through the scenario of a specific ritual performance and reappear in other kinds of ritual, or even transfer from one genre to another, for example, from ritual to a myth-cycle, to an epic, to a fairy tale, to citation as a maxim in a case-at-law. Such a focus leaves the semantic future of each symbol, as it were, open-ended, where formal analysis of a total set of symbols, assumed *a priori* to be a system or a *gestalt*, treated as closed, atemporal, and synchronic, a ''corpus,'' or finite collection of materials, tends to emphasize a given symbol's formal properties and relations and to select from its wealth of meaning only that specific designation which makes it an appropriate term in some binary opposition, itself a relational building block of a bounded cognitive system. Binariness and arbitrariness tend to go together, and both are in the atemporal world of "signifiers." Such a treatment, while often seductively elegant, a *frisson* for our cognitive faculties, removes the total set of symbols from the complex, continuously changing social life, murky or glinting with desire and feeling, which is its distinctive milieu and context, and imparts to it a dualistic *rigor mortis*. Symbols, both as sensorily perceptible vehicles (*signifiants*) and as sets of "meanings" (*signifiés*), are essentially involved in multiple variability, the variability of the essentially living, conscious, emotional, and volitional creatures who employ them not only to give order to the universe they inhabit, but creatively to make use also of disorder, *both* by overcoming or reducing it in particular cases and by its means questioning former axiomatic principles that have become a fetter on the understanding and manipulation of contemporary things. For example, Rabelais's disorderly, scatological heaps of symbolic forms standing for the disorderly deeds and attributes of Gargantua and Pantagruel challenged the neatness of scholastic theological and philosophical systems—the result, paradoxically, was to blast away logically watertight obscurantism. When symbols are rigidified into logical operators and subordinated to implicit syntax-like rules, by some of our modern investigators, those of us who take them too seriously become blind to the creative or innovative potential of symbols as factors in human action. Symbols may "instigate" such action and in situationally varying combinations channel its direction by saturating goals and means with affect and desire. Comparative symbology does attempt to preserve this ludic capacity, to catch symbols in their movement, so to speak, and to "play" with their possibilities of form and meaning. It does this by contextualizing symbols in the concrete, historical fields of their use by "men alive" as they act, react, transact, and interact socially. Even when the symbolic is the *inverse* of the pragmatic reality, it remains intimately in touch with it, affects and is affected by it, provides the positive figure with its negative ground, thereby delimiting each, and winning for "cosmos" a new territory.

Narrower in scope than *semiotics*, comparative symbology is wider than *symbolic anthropology*, for it proposes to take into account not only "ethnographic" materials, but also the symbolic genres of the so-called "advanced" civilizations, the complex, large-scale industrial societies. Undoubtedly, this broader perspective forces it to come to terms with the methods, theories, and findings of specialists and experts in many disciplines which most anthropologists know all too little about, such as history, literature, musicology, art history, theology, the history of religions, philosophy, etc. Nevertheless, in making these attempts to study symbolic action in complex cultures, anthropologists, who now study symbols mainly in "tribal" or simple agrarian myth, ritual, and art, would be doing no more than returning to an honorable tradition of their predecessors, such as Durkheim and the *Anneé Sociologique* school, and Kroeber, Redfield, and their successors, such as Professor Singer, who have examined cultural sub-systems in *oikoumenes* (literally "inhabited worlds," used by Kroeber to indicate civilizational complexes, such as Christendom, Islam, Indic, and Chinese civilization, etc.) and Great Traditions.

In my own case, I was pressed towards the study of symbolic genres in *large*-scale societies by some implications of the work of Arnold van Gennep (which drew principally on the data of small-scale societies) in his *Rites de Passage*, first published in French in 1908. Although van Gennep himself seems to have intended that his term "rite of passage" should be used both for rituals accompanying an individual's or a cohort of individuals' change in social status, and for those associated with seasonal changes for an entire society, his book concentrates on the former type; and the term has come to be used almost exclusively in connection with these "life-crisis" rituals. I have tried to revert to van Gennep's earlier usage in regarding almost *all* types of rites as having the processual form of *"passage."* What does this term mean?

Van Gennep, as is well known, distinguishes three phases in a rite of passage: *separation, transition,* and *incorporation.* The first phase of *separation* clearly demarcates sacred space and time from profane or secular space and time (it is more than just a matter of entering a temple—there must be in addition a rite which changes the quality of *time* also, or constructs a cultural realm which is defined as "out of time," i.e., beyond or outside the time which measures secular processes and routines). It includes symbolic behavior—especially symbols of reversal or inversion of things, relationships and processes secular—which represents the detachment of the ritual subjects (novices, candidates, neophytes or "initiands") from their previous social statuses. In the case of members of a society, it implies collectively moving from all that is socially and culturally involved in an agricultural season, or from a period of peace as against one of war, from plague to community health, from a previous socio-cultural state or condition, to a new state or condition, a new turn of the seasonal wheel. During the intervening phase of *transition*, called by van Gennep "margin" or "limen" (meaning "threshold" in Latin), the ritual subjects pass through a period and area of ambiguity, a sort of social limbo which has few (though sometimes these are most crucial) of the attributes of either the preceding or subsequent profane social statuses or cultural states. We will look at this liminal phase much more closely later. The third phase, called by van Gennep, "reaggregation" or "incorporation" includes symbolic phenomena and actions which represent the return of the subjects to their new, relatively stable, well-defined position in the total society. For those undergoing life-cycle ritual this usually represents an enhanced status, a stage further along life's culturally prefabricated road; for those taking part in a calendrical or seasonal ritual, no change in status may be involved, but they have been ritually prepared for a whole series of changes in the nature of the cultural and ecological activities to be undertaken and of the relationships they will then have with others—all these holding good for a specific quadrant of the annual productive-cycle. Many passage rites are irreversible (for the individual subjects) one shot only affairs, while calendrical rites are repeated every year by everyone, though, of course, one may attend the passage rites of one's kin or friends innumerable times, until one knows their form better than the initiands themselves, like the old ladies who "never miss a wedding" as compared with the nervous couple at their first marriage. I have argued that initiatory passage rites tend to "put people down" while some seasonal rites tend to "set people up," i.e., initiations humble people before permanently elevating them, while some seasonal rites (whose residues are carnivals and festivals) elevate those of low status transiently before returning them to their permanent humbleness. Arnold van Gennep argued that the three phases of his schema varied in length and degree of elaboration in different kinds of passage: for example, "rites of separation are prominent in funeral ceremonies, rites of incorporation at marriages. *Transition* rites may play an important part, for instance, in pregnancy, betrothal, and initiation." The situation is further complicated by regional and ethnic differences which cut across typological ones. Nevertheless, it is rare to find no trace of the three-part schema in "tribal" and "agrarian" rituals.

The passage from one social status to another is often accompanied by a parallel passage in space, a geographical movement from one place to another. This may take the form of a mere opening of doors or the literal crossing of a threshold which separates two distinct areas, one associated with the subject's pre-ritual or preliminal status, and the other with his post-ritual or postliminal status. (The army conscript's "two steps forward" when he obeys his first military order may serve as a modern instance of a ritualized move into liminality.) On the other hand, the spatial passage may involve a long, exacting pilgrimage and the crossing of many national frontiers before the subject reaches his goal, the sacred shrine—where paraliturgical action may replicate in microcosm the three-part schema at the shrine itself. Sometimes this spatial symbolism may be the precursor of a real and permanent change of residence or geographical sphere of action, as when, for example, a Nyakusa or Ndembu girl in Africa, after her puberty rites, leaves her natal village to dwell in her husband's, or in certain hunting societies young boys live with their mothers until the time of their initiation rites into adulthood, after which they begin to live with the other hunters of the tribe. Perhaps something of this thinking persists in our own society, when, in large bureaucratic organizations on the national scale, such as the federal government or a major industrial corporation, the university system, etc., promotion in status and salary usually involves movement in space from one city to another, a process described by William Watson in an article in the book, *Closed Systems to Open Minds* (edited by Max Gluckman, 1965) as "spiralism." The "liminoid" phase between leaving one post and taking up another would repay study in terms of comparative symbology, both in regard to the subject (his dreams, fantasies, favorite reading and entertainment) and to those whom he is leaving and joining (their myths about him, treatment of him, etc.). But there will be more of this and of the distinction between "liminal" and "liminoid" later.

According to van Gennep, an extended liminal phase in the initiation rites of tribal societies is frequently marked by the physical separation of the ritual subjects from the rest of society. Thus in certain Australian, Melanesian, and African tribes, a boy undergoing initiation must spend a long period of time living in the bush, cut off from the normal social interactions within the village and household. Ritual symbols of this phase, though some represent inversion of normal reality, characteristically fall into two types: those of effacement and those of ambiguity or paradox. Hence, in many societies the liminal initiands are often considered to be dark, invisible, like the sun or moon in eclipse or the moon between phases, at the "dark of the moon"; they are stripped of names and clothing, smeared with the common earth rendered indistinguishable from animals. They are associated with such general oppositions as life and death, male and female, food and excrement, simultaneously, since they are at once dying from or dead to their former status and life, and being born and growing into new ones. Sharp symbolic inversion of social attributes may characterize separation; blurring and merging of distinctions may characterize liminality.

Thus, the ritual subjects in these rites undergo a "leveling" process, in which signs of their preliminal status are destroyed and signs of their liminal non-status applied. I have mentioned certain indicators of their liminality—absence of clothing and names—other signs include eating or not eating specific foods, disregard of personal appearance, the wearing of uniform clothing, sometimes irrespective of sex. In mid-transition the initiands are pushed as far toward uniformity, structural invisibility, and anonymity as possible.

By way of compensation, the initiands acquire a special kind of freedom, a "sacred power" of the meek, weak, and humble. As van Gennep elaborates:

> During the entire novitiate, the usual economic and legal ties are modified, sometimes broken altogether. The novices are outside society, and society has no power over them, especially since they are

actually [in terms of indigenous beliefs] sacred and holy, and therefore untouchable and dangerous, just as gods would be. Thus, although taboos, as negative rites, erect a barrier between the novices and society, the society is helpless against the novices' undertakings. That is the explanation—the simplest in the world—for a fact that has been noted among a great many peoples and has remained incomprehensible to observers. During the novitiate, the young people can steal and pillage at will or feed and adorn themselves at the expense of the community (1960:114).

The novices are, in fact, temporarily undefined, beyond the normative social structure. This weakens them, since they have no rights over others. But it also liberates them from structural obligations. It places them too in a close connection with non-social or asocial powers of life and death. Hence the frequent comparison of novices with, on the one hand, ghosts, gods, or ancestors, and, on the other, with animals or birds. They are dead to the social world, but alive to the asocial world. Many societies make a dichotomy, explicit or implicit, between sacred and profane, cosmos and chaos, order and disorder. In liminality, profane social relations may be discontinued, former rights and obligations are suspended, the social order may seem to have been turned upside down, but by way of compensation cosmological systems (as objects of serious study) may become of central importance for the novices, who are confronted by the elders, in rite, myth, song, instruction in a secret language, and various non-verbal symbolic genres, such as dancing, painting, clay-molding, wood-carving, masking, etc., with symbolic patterns and structures which amount to teachings about the structure of the cosmos and their culture as a part and product of it, in so far as these are defined and comprehended, whether implicitly or explicitly. Liminality may involve a complex sequence of episodes in sacred space-time, and may also include subversive and ludic (or playful) events. The factors of culture are isolated, in so far as it is possible to do this with multivocal symbols (i.e., with the aid of symbol-vehicles—sensorily perceptible forms) such as trees, images, paintings, dance forms, etc., that are each susceptible not of a single meaning but of many meanings. Then the factors or elements of culture may be recombined in numerous, often grotesque ways, grotesque because they are arrayed in terms of possible or fantasied rather than experienced combinations—thus a monster disguise may combine human, animal, and vegetable features in an "unnatural" way, while the same features may be differently, but equally "unnaturally" combined in a painting or described in a tale. In other words, in liminality people "play" with the elements of the familiar and defamiliarize them. Novelty emerges from unprecedented combinations of familiar elements.

In the 1972 American Anthropological Association Meetings in Toronto,

Brian Sutton-Smith borrowed a term which I had earlier applied to "liminality" (and other social phenomena and events), namely, "anti-structure" (meaning by this the dissolution of normative social structure, with its role-sets, statuses, jural rights and duties, etc.) and related it to a series of experimental studies he has been making of children's (and some adult) games both in tribal and industrial societies. Much of what he says, *mutatis mutandis,* can be transferred back to the study of liminality in tribal ritual. He writes: "The normative structure represents the working equilibrium, the 'antistructure' represents the latent system of potential alternatives from which novelty will arise when contingencies in the normative system require it. We might more correctly call this second system the *protostructural* system [he says] because it is the precursor of innovative normative forms. It is the source of new culture" (pp. 18-19). Sutton-Smith, who has been recently examining the continuum *order-disorder* in games (such as the English children's game ring-a-ring-a-roses), goes on to say that "we may be disorderly in games [and, I would add, in the liminality of rituals, as well as in such "liminoid" phenomena as charivaris, fiestas, Halloween masking, and mumming, etc.] either because we have an overdose of order, and want to let off steam [this might be called the "conservative view" of ritual disorder, such as ritual reversals, Saturnalia, and the like], or because we have something to *learn* through being disorderly" (p. 17). What interests me most about Sutton-Smith's formulations is that he sees liminal and liminoid situations as the settings in which new models, symbols, paradigms, etc., arise—as the seedbeds of cultural creativity in fact. These new symbols and constructions then feed back into the "central" economic and politico-legal domains and arenas, supplying them with goals, aspirations, incentives, structural models and *raisons d'etre.*

Some have argued, notably the Gallostructuralists of France, that liminality, more specifically "liminal" phenomena such as myth and ritual in tribal society, is best characterized by the establishment of "implicit syntax-like rules" or by "internal structures of logical relations of opposition and mediation between discrete symbolic elements" of the myth or ritual. Claude Lévi-Strauss would perhaps take this view. But to my mind it is the analysis of culture into factors and their free or "ludic" recombination in any and every possible pattern, however weird, that is of the essence of liminality, liminality *par excellence.* This may be seen if one studies liminal phases of major rituals cross-culturally and cross-temporally. When implicit rules begin to appear which limit the possible combination of factors to certain conventional patterns, designs, or configurations, then, I think, we are seeing the intrusion of normative social structure into what is potentially and in principle a free and experimental region of culture, a region where not only new elements but also new combinatory rules may be introduced—far more readily than in the case of language. This capacity for variation and experiment becomes more clearly dominant in societies in which *leisure* is sharply demarcated from *work,* and especially in all societies which have been shaped by the Industrial Revolution. Various Levi-Straussian models, such as the one dealing with metaphorical and opposi-tional logical relations and the transformation to humanity, from nature to culture, and the geometric model which utilizes two sets of oppositions in the construction of a "culinary triangle," raw/cooked:raw/rotten seem to me to be applicable mainly to tribal or early agrarian societies where work and life tend to be governed by seasonal and ecological rhythms, and where the rules underlying the generation of cultural patterns tend to seek out the binary "Yin-Yang," forms suggested by simple "natural" oppositions, such as hot/cold, wet/dry, cultivated/wild, male/female, summer/winter, plenty/scarcity, right/left, sky/earth, above/below and the like. The main social and cultural structures tend to become modeled on these and similar cosmological principles, which determine even the layout of cities and villages, the design of houses, and the shape and spatial placement of dif-ferent types of cultivated land. Analysis of spatial symbolism in relation to cosmological and mythological models has indeed become quite a thriving Gallostructuralist industry lately. It is not surprising that liminality itself cannot escape the grip of these strong structuring principles. Only certain types of *children's* games and play are allowed some degree of freedom because these are defined as structurally "irrelevant," not "mattering." When children are initiated into the early grades of adulthood, however, variabilities and liabilities of social behavior are drastically curtailed and controlled. Children's games cease to be pediarchic·and become pedagogic. Law, morality, ritual, even much of economic life, fall under the structur-ing influence of cosmological principles. The cosmos becomes a complex weave of "correspondences" based on analogy, metaphor and metonomy. For example, the Dogon of West Africa, according to Marcel Griaule, Genevieve Calame Griaule, and Germaine Dieterlen, establish a cor-respondence between the different categories of minerals and the organs of the body. The various soils are conceived of as the organs of "the interior of the stomach," rocks are regarded as the "bones" of the skeleton, and various hues of red clay are likened to "the blood." Similarly, in Medieval China, different ways of painting trees and clouds are related to different cosmological principles.

Thus the symbols found in *rites de passage* in these societies, though sub-ject to permutations and transformations of their relationships, are only in-volved in these *within* relatively stable, cyclical, and repetitive systems. It is to these kinds of systems that the term "liminality" properly belongs. When used of processes, phenomena, and persons in large-scale complex societies, its use must in the main be metaphorical. That is, the word "liminality," used *primarily* of a phase in the processual structure of a *rite de passage,* is applied to other aspects of culture—here in societies of far greater scale and complexity. This brings me to a watershed division in comparative symbology. Failure to distinguish between symbolic systems and genres belonging to cultures which have developed before and after the Industrial Revolution can lead to much confusion both in theoretical treatment and in operational methodology.

Let me try to spell this out. Despite immense diversities within each camp, there still remains a fundamental distinction at the level of expressive culture between all societies before and all societies subsequent to the Industrial Revolution, including the industrializing Third World societies which, although dominantly agrarian, nevertheless represent the granaries or playgrounds of metropolitan industrial societies.

Key concepts here are *work, play,* and *leisure.* Placing a different explanatory stress on each or any combination of these can influence how we think about symbolic manipulation sets, symbolic genres, in the types of societies we will consider. Each of these concepts is multivocal or multivalent, it has many designations. Take *work.* According to the Oxford English Dictionary, "work" means: (1) expenditure of energy, striving, application of effort to some purpose (which fits fairly well with Webster's primary sense: "physical or mental effort exerted to do or to make something; purposeful activity; labor; toil); (2) task to be undertaken, materials to be used in task; (3) thing done, achievement, thing made, books or piece of literary or musical composition [not this application of "work" to the genres of the leisure domain], *meritorious act* as opposed to faith or grace; (5) *employment,* especially the opportunity of earning money by labor, laborious occupation; (6) ordinary, practical (as in *workaday*), etc. [where it has resonances with secular, profane, pragmatic, etc.]. Now in "tribal," "preliterate," "simpler," "small-scale" societies, ritual, and to some extent, myth, are regarded as "work," precisely in this sense, what the Tikopia call "the *work* of the Gods." Ancient Hindu society also posits a "divine work." In the third chapter of the *Bhagavad Gita* (v. 14-15) we find a conection made between sacrifice and work: "From food do all contingent beings derive, and food derives from rain; rain derives from sacrifice and sacrifice from *work.* From Brahman work arises." Nikhilananda comments that "work" here refers to the sacrifice prescribed in the Vedas, which prescribes for "householders," sacrifice or work ("action"). The Ndembu call what a ritual specialist does, *kuzata,* "work," and the same general term is applied to what a hunter, a cultivator, a headman, and, today, a manual laborer, does. Even in fairly complex agrarian societies associated with city-state or feudal polities, well within the scope of historical documentation, we find terms like *liturgy* which in pre-Christian Greece early became established as "public service to the gods." "Liturgy" is derived from the Greek *leos* or *laos,* "the people," and *"ergon,"* *"work"* (cognate with Old English *weorc,* German *werk,* from the Indo-European base, *werg-,* "to do, act." The Greek *organon,* "tool, instrument" derives from the same base—originally *worganon*). The work of men is thus the work of the Gods, a conclusion which would have delighted Durkheim, though it could be construed as implying a fundamental distinction between gods and men, since men cooperated in ritual the better to enter into reciprocal, exhange relations with the gods or with God—it was not simply that "the voice of the congregation was the voice of God." A difference was construed beteen creator and created. Whatever may have been the empirical case, what we are seeing here is a universe or work, an *ergon-* or *organic* universe, in which the main distinction is between sacred and profane *work,* not between work and leisure. For example, Samuel Beal comments in his *Travels of Fah-Hian Sung-Yun, Buddhist Pilgrim from China to India* (A.D. 600 and A.D. 518), [1964: p. 4 ff.], on Chi Fah-Hian's use of the term "shaman," as follows: "The Chinese word *shaman* represents phonetically the Sanscrit *sramana,* or the Pali *samana.* The Chinese word is defined to mean 'diligent,' 'laborious.' The Sanscrit root is '*sram,*' to be fatigued." (He was referring to the people of Shen-Shen, in the desert of Makhai, part of the Gobi Desert region.) It is, furthermore, a universe of work in which whole communities participate, as of obligation, not optation. The *whole* community goes through the *entire* ritual round, whether in terms of total or representative participation. Thus, some rites, such as those of sowing, first fruits, or harvest, may involve everyone, man, woman, and child, others may be focused on specific groups, categories, associations, etc., such as men *or* women, old *or* young, one clan *or* another, one association or secret society *or* another. Yet the whole ritual round adds up to the total participation of the whole community. Sooner or later, no one is exempt from ritual duty, just as no one is exempt from economic, legal, or political duty. Communal participation, obligation, the passage of the whole society through crises, collective and individual, directly or by proxy, are the hallmarks of "the work of the gods" and sacred human work—without which profane human work would be, for the community, impossible to conceive, though no doubt, as history has cruelly demonstrated to those conquered by industrial societies, possible to live, or, at least, exist through.

Yet it can be argued that this "work" is not work, as we in industrial societies know it, but has in both its dimensions, sacred and profane, an element of "play." Insofar as the community and its individual members regard themselves as the masters or "owners" of ritual and liturgy, or as representatives of the ancestors and gods who ultimately "own" them, they have authority to introduce, under certain culturally determined conditions, elements of novelty from time to time into the socially inherited deposit of ritual customs. Liminality, the seclusion period, is a phase peculiarly conducive to such "ludic" invention. Perhaps it would be better to regard the distinction between "work" and "play," or better between "work" and "leisure" (which includes but exceeds play *sui generis*), as itself an artifact of the Industrial Revolution, and to see such symbolic-expressive genres as ritual and myth as being at once work and play or at least as cultural activities in which work and play are intricately inter-calibrated. Yet it often happens that the historically *later* can throw light on the *earlier*, especially when there is a demonstrable sociogenetic connection between them. For there are undoubtedly "ludic" aspects in "tribal," etc., culture, especially in the liminal periods of protracted initiation or calen-drically based rituals. Such would include joking relationships, sacred games, such as the ball games of the ancient Maya and modern Cherokee, riddles, mock-ordeals, holy fooling, and clowning, Trickster tales told in liminal times and places, in or out of ritual contexts, and host of other types.

The point is though, that these play or ludic aspects of tribal agrarian ritual myth are, as Durkheim says, "de la vie sérieuse," i.e., they are in-trinsically connected with the "work" of the collectivity in performing sym-bolic actions and manipulating symbolic objects so as to promote and in-crease fertility of men, crops, and animals, domestic and wild, to cure ill-ness, to avert plague, to obtain success in raiding, to turn boys into men and girls into women, to make chiefs out of commoners, to transform or-dinary people into shamans and shamanins, to "cool" those "hot" from the warpath, to ensure the proper succession of seasons and the hunting and agricultural responses of human beings to them, and so forth. Thus, the play is in earnest, and has to be within bounds. For example, in the Ndembu Twin Ritual, *Wubwang'u*, described in *The Ritual Process*, in one episode women and men abuse one another verbally in a highly sexual and jocose way. Much personal inventiveness goes into the invective, though much is also stylized. Nevertheless, this ludic behavior is pressed into the service of the ultimate aim of the ritual—to produce healthy offspring, but not *too many* healthy offspring at once. Abundance is good, but reckless abundance is a foolish joke. Hence cross-sexual joking both maintains reasonable fertility and restrains unreasonable fecundity. Joking is fun, but it is also a social sanction. Even joking must observe the "golden mean," which is an ethical feature of "cyclical, repetitive societies," not as yet un-balanced by innovative ideas and technical changes. Technical innovations are the products of ideas, the products of which I will call the "*liminoid*" (the "-oid" here derives from Greek-*eidos,* a form, shape; and means "like, resembling"; "liminoid" *resembles* without being identical with "liminal") and what Marx assigned to a domain he called "the *super*structural"—I would prefer to talk about the "*anti-,*" "*meta-,*" or "*proto*structural." "Superstructural," for Marx, has the connotation of a distorted mirroring, even falsification or mystification of the "structural" or "infrastructural" which is, in his terms, the constellation of productive relations, both in cohesion and conflict. Contrarily, I see the "liminoid" as an independent and critical source—like the liminoid "works" of Marx, written in the secluded space of the British Museum Library—and here we observe how "liminoid" actions of industrial leisure genres can repossess the character of "work" though originating in a "free time" arbitrarily separated by managerial fiat from the time of "labor"—how the liminoid can be an independent domain of creative activity, not simply a distorted mirror-image, mask, or cloak for structural activity in the "centers" or "mainstreams" of "productive social labor." To call them a distorting mirror is to identify liminoid productions solely with apologia for the political *status quo*. "Antistructure," in fact, can generate and store a plurality of alternative models for living, from utopias to programs, which are capable of influencing the behavior of those in mainstream social and political roles (whether authoritative or dependent, in control or rebelling against it) in the direction of radical change, just as much as they can serve as instruments of politcal control. As scientists we are interested in demarcating a domain, not in taking sides with one or other of the groups or categories which operate within it. Experimental and theoretical science itself is "liminoid"—it takes place in "neutral spaces" or privileged areas—laboratories and studies—set aside from the mainstream of productive or political events. Universities, institutes, colleges, etc., are "liminoid" settings for all kinds of freewheeling, experimental cognitive behavior as well as forms of symbolic action, resembling some found in tribal society, like "rushing" and "pledging" ceremonies in American college fraternity and society houses, for example. This, of course, does not mean that liminoid products have no political significance: think of the Rights of Man and the *Communist Manifesto*, for example. Or Plato's *Republic* or Hobbes's *Leviathan*.

But let's look more closely at this notion of the "liminoid," and try to distinguish it from the "liminal." To do this properly, we have to examine the notion of "play." Etymology does not tell us too much about its meaning. We learn that the word "play" is derived from OE *plegan,* "to exercise oneself, move briskly," and that the Middle Dutch *pleyen,* "to dance," is a cognate term. Walter Skeat, in his *Concise Etymological Dictionary of the English Language* (p. 355), suggests that the Anglo-Saxon *plega,* "a game, sport," is also (commonly) "a fight, a battle." He considers, too, that the Anglo-Saxon terms are borrowed from the Latin *plaga,* "a stroke." Even if the idea of a "danced-out or ritualized fight" gets into subsequent denotations of "play," this multivocal concept has its own historical destiny.

For *Webster's Dictionary,* play is: (1) action, motion, or activity, esp. when free, rapid, or light (e.g., the *play* of muscles)—here, as so often, "play" is conceived as "light" as against the "heaviness" of "work," "free" as against work's "necessary" or "obligatory" character, "rapid" as against the careful, reflected-upon style of work routines; (2) "freedom or scope for motion or action"; (3) "activity engaged in for amusement or recreation"—here, again, we are verging on the notion of activities disengaged from necessity or obligation; (4) "fun, joking (to do a thing in *play*)"—emphasizing the *non*-serious character of certain types of modern play; (5) (a) "the playing of a game," (b) "the way or technique of playing a game"—here reintroducing the notion that play might be work, might be serious within its non-serious dimension, and raising the problem of what are the conditions under which "fun" becomes "technique" and rule-governed; (6) (a) "a maneuver, move, or act in a game" (e.g., the "wishbone" or "T" offensive formation in American football or a specific brilliant move by a team or individual), (b) "a turn at playing" (e.g., "there's one play left in the game"); (7) "the act of gambling" (and here we may think of the "gambling" character of divination in tribal and even in feudal society, and, of course, the very word "gamble" is derived from OE *gamenian*, "to play" akin to the German dialect term *gammeln*, "to sport, make merry"; (8) "a dramatic composition or performance; drama," "the play's the thing"—clearly this term preserves something of the earlier sense of "fight, battle" as well as those of "recreation," "technique," and "turns (i.e., acts, scenes, etc.) at playing"; (9) finally, "play" can mean "sexual activity, dalliance." Here again we can see a shift from the meaning of sex as procreative "work," (a persistent meaning often supported by religious doctrine in tribal and feudal societies) to the division of sexual activity into "play" or "foreplay," and the "serious" business or "work" of begetting progeny. Post-industrial birth control techniques make this division practically realizable, and themselves exemplify the division between work and play brought about by modern systems of production and thought, both "objectively," in the domain of culture, and "subjectively" in the individual conscience and consciousness. The distinction between "subjective" and "objective" may itself be partly an artifact of the sundering of work and play. For "work" is held to be the realm of the rational adaptation of means to ends, of "objectivity," while "play" is thought of as divorced from this essentially "objective" realm, and, in so far as it is its inverse, it is "subjective," free from external constraints, where any and every combination of variable can be "played" with. Indeed, Jean Piaget, who has done most to study the developmental psychology of play, regards it as "a kind of free assimilation, without accommodation to spatial conditions or to the significance of objects." (*Play, Dream, and Imitation*, 1962, p. 86).

In the liminal phases and states of tribal and agrarian cultures—in ritual, myth, and legal processes—work and play are hardly distinguishable in many cases. Thus, in Vedic India, according to Alain Danielou (*Hindu*

Polytheism, 1964:144), the "gods [*sura* and *deva*, who are objects of serious sacrificial ritual] play. The rise, duration and destruction of the world is their game." Ritual is both earnest and playful. As Milton Singer has pointed out in his book on contemporary India, *When a Great Tradition Modernizes* (p. 160), the "Krishna dance" in an urban *bhajana* program (group hymn singing) is called *lila*, "sport," in which the participants "play" at being the "Gopis" or cowherdesses who "sport" in a variety of ways with Krishna, Vishnu incarnate, reliving the myth. But the Gopis' erotic love-play with Krishna has mystical implications, like the *Song of Solomon*—it is at once serious and playful, God's "sport" with a human soul.

Now let us consider the clear division between *work* and *leisure* which modern industry has produced, and how this has affected all symbolic genres, from ritual to games and literature. Joffre Dumazedier, of the Centre d'Etudes Sociologiques (Paris), is not the only authority who holds that leisure "has certain traits that are characteristic only of the civilization born from the industrial revolution" (*International Encyclopedia of the Social Sciences*, article on "Leisure," 1968:248-253, also *Le Loisir et La Ville*, 1962). But he puts the case very pithily and I am beholden to his argument. Dumazedier dismisses the view that leisure has existed in all societies at all times. In archaic and tribal societies, he maintains, "work and play alike formed part of the ritual by which men sought communion with the ancestral spirits. Religious festivals embodied both work and play" (p. 248). Yet religious specialists such as shamans and medicine-men did not constitute a "leisure class" in Thorstein Veblen's sense, since they performed religious or magical functions for the whole community (and, as we have seen, shamanism is a "diligent and laborious" profession). Similarly, in the agricultural societies of recorded history, "the working year followed a timetable written in the very passage of the days and seasons: in good weather work was hard, in bad weather it slackened off. Work of this kind had a natural rhythm to it, punctuated by rests, songs, games, and ceremonies; it was synonymous with the daily round, and in some regions began at sunrise, to finish only at sunset . . . the cycle of the year was also marked by a whole series of sabbaths and feast days. The sabbath belonged to religion; feast days, however, were often occasions for a great investment of energy (not to mention food) and constituted the obverse or opposite of everyday life [often characterized by symbolic inversion and status reversal]. But the ceremonial [or ritual] aspect of these celebrations could not be disregarded; they stemmed from religion [defined as sacred *work*], not leisure [as we think of it today] . . . They were imposed by religious requirements . . . [and] the major European civilizations knew more than 150 workless days a year" (p. 249).

Sebastian de Grazia has argued (*Of Time, Work, and Leisure*, 1962) that the origins of leisure can be traced to the way of life enjoyed by certain aristocratic classes in the course of Western civilization. Dumazedier disagrees, pointing out the idle state of Greek philosophers and sixteenth century gentry cannot be defined *in relation to* work, but rather *replaces work altogether*. Work is done by slaves, peasants, or servants. True leisure only exists when it complements or rewards work. This is not to say that many of the refinements of human culture did not come from this aristocratic idleness. Dumazedier thinks that it is significant that the Greek word for having nothing to do (*schole*) also meant "school." "The courtiers of Europe, after the end of the Middle Ages, both invented and extolled the ideal of the humanist and the gentleman" (p. 249).

"Leisure," then, presupposes "work": it is a non-work, even an anti-work phase in the life of a person who also works. If we were to indulge in terminological neophily, we might call it *anergic* as against *ergic*. Leisure arises, says Dumazedier, under two conditions. First, society ceases to govern its activities by means of common ritual obligations: some activities, including work and leisure, become, at least in theory, *subject to individual choice*. Secondly, the work by which a person earns his or her living is "set apart from his other activities: its limits are no longer 'natural' but arbitrary—indeed, it is organized in so definite a fashion that it can easily be separated, both in theory and in practice, from his free time." It is only in the social life of industrial and postindustrial civilizations that we find these necessary conditions. Other social theorists, both radical and conservative, have pointed out that leisure is the product of industrialized, rationalized, bureaucratized, large-scale socio-economic systems with arbitrary rather than natural delimitation of "work" from "free time" or "time out." Work is now organized by industry so as to be separated from "free time," which includes, in addition to leisure, attendance to such personal needs as eating, sleeping, and caring for one's health and appearance, as well as familial, social, civic, political, and religious obligations (which would have fallen within the domain of the work-play continuum in tribal society). Leisure is predominantly an urban phenomenon, so that when the concept of leisure begins to penetrate rural societies, it is because agricultural labor is tending towards an industrial, "rationalized" mode of organization, and because rural life is becoming permeated by the urban values of industrialization—this holds good for the "Third World" today as well as for the rural hinterlands of long-established industrial societies.

Leisure-time is associated with two types of freedom, "freedom-from" and "freedom-to," to advert to Isaiah Berlin's famous distinction. (1) It represents *freedom from* a whole heap of institutional obligations prescribed by the basic forms of social, particularly technological and bureaucratic, organization. (2) For each individual, it means *freedom from* the forced, chronologically regulated rhythms of factory and office and a chance to recuperate and enjoy natural, biological rhythms again.

Leisure is also: (1) *freedom to* enter, even to generate new symbolic worlds of entertainment, sports, games, diversions of all kinds. It is, furthermore, (2) *freedom to* transcend social structural limitations, freedom to *play* . . . with ideas, with fantasies, with words (from Rabelais to Joyce and Samuel Beckett), with paint (from the Impressionists to Action painting and Art Nouveau), and with social relationships—in friendship, sensitivity training, psychodramas, and in other ways. Here far more than in tribal or agrarian rites and ceremonies, the ludic and the experimental are stressed. In complex, organic-solidary societies, there are obviously many more options: games of skill, strength, and chance can serve as models for future behavior or models of past work experience—now viewed as release from work's necessities and something one chooses to do. Sports like football, games like chess, recreations like mountaineering can be hard and exacting and governed by rules and routines even more stringent than those of the work situation, but, since they are optional, they are part of an individual's freedom, of his growing self-mastery, even self-transcendence. Hence, they are imbued more thoroughly with pleasure than those many types of industrial work in which men are alienated from the fruits and results of their labor. Leisure is potentially capable of releasing creative powers, individual or communal, either to criticize or buttress the dominant social structural values.

It is certain than no one is committed to a true leisure activity by material needs or by moral or legal obligations, as is the case with the activities of getting an education, earning a living, or carrying out civic or religious ceremonies. Even when there is effort, as in competitive sport, that effort—and the discipline of training—is chosen voluntarily, in the expectation of an enjoyment that is disinterested, unmotivated by gain, and has no utilitarian or ideological purpose.

But if this is ideally the spirit of leisure, the cultural reality of leisure is obviously influenced by the domain of work from which it has been split by the wedge of industrial organization. Work and leisure interact, each individual participates in both realms, and the modes of work organization affect the styles of leisure pursuits. Let's consider the case of those mainly Northern European and North American societies whose preliminary industrialization was accompanied and infused with the spirit of what Max Weber has called "the Protestant Ethic." This ethical milieu, or set of values and beliefs, which Weber thought was an auspicious condition for the growth of modern, rational capitalism, in my view, produced effects in the *leisure* domain quite as far-reaching as in that of work. As everyone now knows, according to Weber, John Calvin and other Protestant reformers taught that salvation is a pure gift from God and cannot be earned or merited by a being so thoroughly depraved in his nature since the Fall of

Adam as man. In its extreme form, Predestination, this meant than no one could be certain of being saved, or indeed of being damned. This threatened seriously to undermine individual morale, and a get-out clause evolved at the level of popular culture, though it could not be made theologically watertight. This was that he who is in God's grace and (invisibly) among the elect by God's foreordaining does actually manifest in his behavior systematic self-control and obedience to the will of God. By these outward signs it may be known to others, and he can reassure himself that he is among the elect, and will not suffer eternal damnation with the reprobate. But the Calvinist is never finally certain that he will be saved and thus dedicates himself to an incessant examination of the conditions of his inward soul and outward life for evident indications of the work of salvific grace. In a sense, what was in cultural history previously the social "work of the Gods," the calendrical, liturgical round, or, rather, its penances and ordeals, not its festive rewards, became "internalized" as the systematic, non-ludic "work" of the individual's conscience.

Another Calvinist emphasis was on the notion of one's calling in life, one's vocation. As against the Catholic notion of "vocation" as the call to a religious life, framed by the traditional vows of chastity, obedience, and poverty, the Calvinist held that it was precisely a person's worldly occupation that must be regarded as the sphere in which he was to serve God through his dedication to his work. Work and leisure were made separate spheres, and "work" became sacred, *de facto,* as the arena in which one's salvation might be objectively demonstrated. Thus, the man of property was to act as as steward of worldly goods, like Joseph in Egypt. He was to use them not for sinful luxury, but to better the moral condition of himself, his family, and his employees. "Betterment" implied self-discipline, self-examination, hard work, dedication to one's duty and calling, and an insistence that those under one's authority should do the same. Wherever the Calvinist aspiration to theocracy became influential, as in Geneva or in the transient dominance of English Puritanism, legislation was introduced to force men to better their spiritual state through thrift and hard work. For example, English Puritanism affected not only religious worship by its attack on "ritualism," but also reduced "ceremonial" ("secular" ritual) to a minimum in many other fields of activity, including drama, which they stigmatized as "mummery." Their Act making stage performances illegal cut twenty odd years from Ben Jonson's playwriting. Among the targets of such legislation, then, were significantly, such genres of leisure entertainment which had developed in aristocratic or mercantilist circles in the proto-industrializing period as theatrical productions, masques, pageants, musical performances, and, of course, the popular genres of carnivals, festivals, charivaris, ballad singing, and miracle plays. These represented the "ludic" face of the work-play continuum that had formerly caught up the whole of society into a single process moving through sacred and pro-fane, solemn and festive phases in the seasonal round. The Calvinists wanted "no more cakes and ale"—or other festival foods that belonged to the work and play of the gods. What they wanted was ascetic dedication to the mainline economic enterprise, the sacralization of what was formerly mostly profane, or, at least, *subordinated to,* ancillary to the sacred cosmological paradigms. Weber argues that when the religious motivations of Calvinism were lost after a few generations of worldly success, the focus on self-examination, self-discipline, and hard work in one's calling even when secularized continued to promote the ascetic dedication to systematic profits, reinvestment of earnings, and thrift which were the hall marks of nascent capitalism.

Something of this systematic, vocational character of the Protestant ethic came to tinge even the entertainment genres of industrial leisure. To coin a term, even leisure became *ergic,* "of the nature of work," rather than *ludic,* of the nature of play. Thus, we have a *serious* division of *labor* in the *entertainment* business, acting, dancing, singing, art, writing, composing, etc., becoming professionalized "vocations." Educational institutions prepared actors, dancers, singers, painters, and authors for their "careers." At a higher level, there grew up in the late eighteenth and especially in the nine-teenth centuries the notion of "art" itself, in its various modalities, as a quasi-religious vocation, with its own asceticism and total dedication, from William Blake, through Kierkegaard, Baudelaire, Lermontov, and Rim-baud, to Cézanne, Proust, Rilke, Joyce, not to mention Beethoven, Mahler, Sibelius, etc., etc.

Another aspect of this influence of the Protestant ethic on leisure is in the realm of play itself. As Edward Norbeck has said ("Man at Play," in *Play, A Natural History Magazine Special Supplement,* December 1971:48-53): "America's forefathers believed strongly in the set of values known as the Protestant ethic. Devotion to work was a Christian virtue; and play, the enemy of work, was reluctantly and charily permitted only to children. Even now, these values are far from extinct in our nation, and the old ad-monition that play is the devil's handiwork continues to live in secular thought. Although play has now become almost respectable, it is still something in which we 'indulge' (as in sexual acts), a form of moral lax-ness." Organized sport ("pedagogic" play) better fits the Puritan tradition than unorganized children's play ("pediarchic" play) or mere dalliance, which is time wasted.

Nevertheless, modern industrial or post-industrial societies have shed many of these anti-leisure attitudes. Technological development, political and industrial organization by workers, action by liberal employers, revolutions in many parts of the world, have had the cumulative effect of bringing more leisure into the "free-time" of industrial cultures. In this leisure, symbolic genres, both of the entertainment and instructive sorts, have proliferated. In my book, *The Ritual Process,* I have spoken of some of these as "liminal" phenomena. In view of what I have just said, is liminality an adequate label for this set of symbolic activities and forms? Clearly, there are some respects in which these "anergic" genres share characteristics with the "ludergic" rituals and myths (if we contrast the Hindu and Judaic ritual style) of archaic, tribal and early agrarian cultures. Leisure can be conceived of as a betwixt-and-between, a neither-this-nor-that domain between two spells of work or between occupational and familial and civic activity. Leisure is etymologically derived from the Old French *leisir,* which itself derives from the Latin *licere,* "to be permitted," and which, interestingly enough, comes from the Indo-European base *leik*—"to offer for sale, bargain," referring to the "liminal" sphere of the market, with its implications of choice, variation, contract—a sphere that has connections, in archaic and tribal religions, with Trickster deities such as Eshu-Elegba, and Hermes. Exchange is more "liminal" than production. Just as when tribesmen make masks, disguise themselves as monsters, heap up disparate ritual symbols, invert or parody profane reality in myths and folk-tales, so do the genres of industrial leisure, the theatre, poetry, novel, ballet, film, sport, rock music, classical music, art, pop art, etc., *play* with the factors of culture, sometimes assembling them in random, grotesque, improbable, surprising, shocking, usually experimental combinations. But they do this in a much more complicated way than in the liminality of tribal initiations, multiplying specialized genres of artistic and popular entertainments, mass culture, pop culture, folk culture, high culture, counterculture, underground culture, etc., as against the relatively limited symbolic genres of "tribal" society, and within each allowing lavish scope to authors, poets, dramatists, painters, sculptors, composers, musicians, actors, comedians, folksingers, rock musicians, "makers" generally, to generate not only weird forms, but also, and not infrequently, models, direct and parabolic or aesopian, that are highly critical of the *status quo* as a whole or in part. Of course, given *diversity* as a *principle,* many artists, in many genres, also buttress, reinforce, justify, or otherwise seek to legitimate the prevailing social and cultural mores and political orders. Those that do so, do so in ways that tend more closely than the *critical* productions to parallel tribal myths and rituals—they are "liminal" or "pseudo-" or "post-" "liminal," rather than "liminoid." Satire is a conservative genre because it is *pseudo-liminal.* Satire exposes, attacks, or derides what it considers to be vices, follies, stupidities, or abuses, but its criterion of judgment is usually the normative structural frame of officially promulgated values. Hence satirical works, like those of Swift, Castlereagh, or Evelyn Waugh, often have a "ritual of reversal" form, indicating that disorder is no permanent substitute for order. A mirror inverts but also reflects an object. It does not break it down into constituents in order to remold it, far less does it annihilate and replace that object. But art and literature often do precisely these things, if only in the realm of imagination. The *liminal* phases of tribal society invert but do not usually subvert the *status quo,* the structural form, of society; reversal underlines to the members of a community that chaos is the alternative to cosmos, so they'd better stick to cosmos, i.e., the traditional order of culture, though they can for a brief while have a whale of a good time being chaotic, in some saturnalian or lupercalian revelry, some charivari, or institutionalized orgy. But supposedly "entertainment" genres of industrial society are often *subversive,* satirizing, lampooning, burlesquing, or subtly putting down the central values of the basic, work-sphere society, or at least of selected sectors of that society. The word "entertain," incidentally, is derived from O.F. *entretenir,* to "hold apart," that is, to create a liminal or liminoid space in which performances may take place. Some of these entertainment genres, such as the "legitimate" or "classical" theatre, are historically continuous with ritual, as in the cases of Greek tragedy or Japanese *Noh* theatre, and possess something of the sacred seriousness, even the *rites de passage* structure of their antecedents. Nevertheless, crucial differences separate the structure, function, style, scope and symbology of the *liminal* in tribal and agrarian ritual and myth from what we may perhaps call the "liminoid," or leisure genres, of symbolic forms and action in complex, industrial societies. I shall soon go on to discuss some of these differences.

The term *limen* itself, the Latin for "threshold," selected by van Gennep to apply to "transition between," appears to be negative in connotation, since it is no longer the positive past condition nor yet the positive articulated future condition. It seems, too, to be passive since it is dependent on the articulated, positive conditions it mediates. Yet on probing one finds in liminality both positive and active qualities, especially where that "threshold" is protracted and becomes a "tunnel," when the "liminal" becomes the "cunicular"; this is particularly the case in initiation rituals, with their long periods of seclusion and training of novices rich in the deployment of symbolic forms and esoteric teachings. "Meaning" in culture tends to be *generated* at the interfaces between established cultural subsystems, though meanings are then institutionalized and consolidated at the centers of such systems. Liminality is a temporal interface whose properties partially invert those of the already consolidated order which constitutes any specific cultural "cosmos." It may be useful heuristically to consider in relation to liminality in ritual/myth Durkheim's overall characterization of "mechanical solidarity," which he regarded as that type of cohesion plus cooperative, collective action directed towards the achievement of group goals which best applies to small, non-literate societies with a simple division of labor, and very little tolerance of individuality. He based this type of solidarity on a *homogeneity* of values and behavior, strong social constraint, and loyalty to tradition and kinship. The rules for togetherness are known and shared. Now what frequently typifies the liminality of initiation ritual in societies with mechanical solidarity is precisely the opposite of this: ordeals, myths, maskings, mumming, the presentation of sacred icons to novices, secret languages, food and behavioral taboos, create a weird domain in the seclusion camp in which ordinary regularities of kinship, the residential setting, tribal law and custom are set aside, where the bizarre becomes the normal, and where through the loosening of connections between elements customarily bound together in certain combinations, their scrambling and recombining in monstrous, fantastic, and unnatural shapes, the novices are induced to think, and think hard, about cultural experiences they had hitherto taken for granted. The novices are taught that they did not know what they thought they knew. Beneath the surface structure of custom was a deep structure, whose rules they had to learn, through paradox and shock. In some ways social constraints become stronger, even unnaturally and irrationally stronger, as when the novices are compelled by their elders to undertake what in their minds are unnecessary tasks by arbitrary fiat, and punished severely if they fail to obey promptly, and, what is worse, even if they succeed. But in other ways, as in the case cited earlier from van Gennep's *Rites de Passage,* the novices also are conceded unprecedented freedoms—they make raids and swoops on villages and gardens, seize women, vituperate older people. Innumerable are the forms of topsy-turveydom, parody, abrogation of the normative system, exaggeration of rule into caricature or satirizing of rule. The novices are at once put outside and inside the circle of the previously known. But one thing must be kept in mind—*all* these acts and symbols are of *obligation.* Even the *breaking* of rules *has* to be done during initiation. This is one of the distinctive ways in which the liminal is marked off from the liminoid. In the 1972 American Anthropological Association Meetings in Toronto, several examples were cited (among them, the carnival in St. Vincent in the West Indies, and La Have Islands, Nova Scotia, cited by R. Abrahams and R. Bauman, 1972) from modern societies on the fringe of industrial civilizations which bore some resemblance to liminal inversions in tribal societies. But what struck me was how even in these "out-back" regions *optionality* dominated the whole process. For example, when the masked mummers of La Have, usually older boys and young married men, known as "belsnicklers," emerge on Christmas Eve to entertain, tease, and fool adults, and to frighten children, they knock at house doors and windows, asking to be "allowed" entrance. Some householders actually refuse to let them in. Now I cannot imagine a situation in which Ndembu, Luvale, Chokwe, or Luchazi masked dancers (peoples I have known and observed),

who emerge after the performance of a certain ritual, marking the end of
one half of the seclusion period and the beginning of another in the circumcision ritual known as *Mukanda,* and approach to dance in villages and
threaten women and children, would be refused entry. Nor do they ask per-
mission to enter; they storm in! Belsnicklers have to "ask for" treats from
householders. *Makishi* (maskers) among Ndembu, etc., demand food and
gifts as of right. Optation pervades the liminoid phenomenon, obligation
the liminal. One is all play and choice, an entertainment, the other is a matter of deep seriousness, even dread, it is demanding, compulsory, though,
indeed, fear provokes nervous laughter from the women (who, if touched
by the *makishi,* are believed to contract leprosy, become sterile, or go mad!).
Again, in St. Vincent, only *certain types* of personalities are attracted to the
carnival as performers, those whom R. Abrahams, the investigator,
describes as "the rude and sporty segment of the community," who are
"rude and sporty" *whenever* they have an opportunity to be so, all year
round—hence can most aptly personify "disorder" versus "order" at the
carnival. Here, again, optation is evidently dominant—for people do not
have to act invertedly—as in tribal rituals; some people, but not *all* people,
choose to act invertedly at the carnival. And the carnival is unlike a tribal
ritual in that it can be attended *or* avoided, performed or merely watched,
at *will.* It is a genre of leisure enjoyment, not an obligatory ritual, it is play-
separated-from-work, not play-and-work ludergy as a binary system of
man's "serious" communal endeavor. Abrahams, in his joint paper with
Bauman, makes a further valid point, which firmly places Vincentian carnivals in the modern-leisure-genre category, when he stresses that it is over-
whelmingly the "bad, unruly (*macho*-type) men," who choose to perform
carnival inversions indicative of disorder in the universe and society, people who are disorderly by temperament and choice in many, extra-carnival
situations. To the contrary, in tribal ritual, even the normally orderly,
meek, and "law-abiding" people would be *obliged* to be disorderly in key
rituals, regardless of their temperament and character. The sphere of the
optional is in such societies much reduced. Even in liminality, where the
bizarre behavior so often remarked upon by anthropologists occurs, the
sacra, masks, etc., emerge to view under the guise at least of "collective
representations." If there ever were individual creators and artists, they
have been subdued by the general "liminal" emphasis on anonymity and
commmunitas, just as the novices and their novice-masters have been. But
in the liminoid genres of industrial art, literature, and even science (more
truly homologous with tribal liminal thinking than modern art), great
public stress is laid on the individual innovator, the unique person who
dares and opts to create. In this lack of stress on individuality, tribal
liminality may be seen not as the inverse of tribal normativeness, but as its
projection into ritual situations. However, this has to be modified when one
looks at actual initiation rituals "on the ground." I found that, among the

Ndembu, despite the novices' being stripped of names, profane rank, clothes, each emerged as a distinct individual and there was an element of competitive personal distinctiveness in the fact that the best four novices in the terms of performance during seclusion—in hunting, endurance of ordeal, smartness in answering riddles, cooperativeness, etc.—were given titles in the rites marking their reaggregation to profane society. For me, this indicated that in liminality is secreted the seed of the liminoid, waiting only for major changes in the sociocultural context to set it agrowing into the branched "candelabra" of manifold liminoid cultural genres. If one *has to,* like Tom Thumb, in the English nursery rhyme, pull out a dialectical plum, from each and every type of social formation, I would counsel that investigators who propose to study one of the world's fast disappearing "tribal" societies should look at the liminal phases of their rituals in order most precisely to locate the incipient contradiction between communal-anonymous and private-distinctive modes of conceiving principals of sociocultural growth.

I have used the term "anti-structure," mainly with reference to tribal and agrarian societies, to describe both liminality and what I have called "communitas." I meant by it not a structural reversal, a mirror-imaging of "profane" workaday socioeconomic structure, or a fantasy-rejection of structural "necessities," but the liberation of human capacities of cognition, affect, volition, creativity, etc., from the normative constraints incumbent upon occupying a sequence of social statuses, enacting a multiplicity of social roles, and being acutely conscious of membership in some corporate group such as a family, lineage, clan, tribe, nation, etc., or of affiliation with some pervasive social category such as a class, caste, sex or age-division. Sociocultural systems drive so steadily towards consistency that human individuals only get off these normative hooks in rare situations in small-scale societies, and not too frequently in large-scale ones. Nevertheless, the exigencies of structuration itself, the process of containing new growth in orderly patterns or schemata, has an Achilles heel. This is the fact that when persons, groups, sets of ideas, etc., move from one level or style of organization or regulation of the interdependence of their parts or elements to another level, there has to be an interfacial region or, to change the metaphor, an interval, however brief, of *margin* or *limen*, when the past is momentarily negated, suspended, or abrogated, and the future has not yet begun, an instant of pure potentiality when everything, as it were, trembles in the balance. (Like the trembling quarterback with all the "options" but with the very solid future moving menacingly towards him!) In tribal societies, due to the general overriding homogeneity of values, behavior, and social structural rules, this instant can be fairly easily contained or dominated by social structure, held in check from innovative excess, "hedged about," as anthropologists delight to say, by "taboos," "checks and balances," etc. Thus, the tribal liminal, however exotic in appearance, can never be much more than a subversive flicker. It is put into the service of normativeness almost as soon as it appears. Yet I see it as a kind of institutional capsule or pocket which contains the germ of future social developments, of societal change, in a way that the central tendencies of a social system can never quite succeed in being, the spheres where law and custom, and the modes of social control ancillary to these, prevail. Innovation can take place in such spheres, but most frequently it occurs in interfaces and limina, then becomes *legitimated* in central sectors. For me, such relatively "late" social processes, historically speaking, as "revolution," "insurrection," and even "romanticism" in art, characterized by freedom in form and spirit, emphasis on feeling and originality, represent an inversion of the relation between the normative and the liminal in "tribal" and other essentially conservative societies. For in these modern processes and movements, the seeds of cultural transformation, discontent with the way things are culturally, and social criticism, always implicit in the preindustrially liminal, have become situationally central, no longer a matter of the interface between "fixed structures" but a matter of the holistically developmental. Thus revolutions, whether successful or not, become the *limina*, with all their initiatory overtones, between major distinctive structural forms or orderings of society. It may be that this is to use "liminal" in a metaphorical, not in the "primary" or "literal" sense advocated by van Gennep, but this usage may help us to think about global human society, to which all specific historical social formations may well be converging. Revolutions, whether violent or non-violent, may be the totalizing liminal phases for which the limina of tribal *rites de passage* were merely foreshadowings or premonitions.

This may possibly be the point where we should feed.in the other major variable of the "antistructural," communitas. (I will discuss the merits and demerits of talking about "antistructure," "metastructure" and "protostructure" later.) There is in tribal societies probably a closer relationship between communitas and liminality than between communitas and normative structure, though the modality of human interrelatedness which is communitas can "play" across structural systems in a way too difficult for us at present to predict its motions—this is the experiential basis, I believe, of the Christian notion of "actual grace." Thus, in the workshop, village, office, lecture-room, theatre, almost anywhere people can be subverted from their duties and rights into an atmospere of communitas. What then *is* communitas? Has it any reality base, or is it a persistent fantasy of mankind, a sort of collective return to the womb? I have described this way by which persons see, understand, and act towards one another (in *The Ritual Process*) as essentially "an unmediated relationship between historical, idiosyncratic, concrete individuals." This is *not* the same as Georges Gurvitch's notion of "communion" which he describes ("Mass, Community, Communion" in *J. of Philosophy*, August 1941:489) as "when minds open out as widely as possible and the least accessible depths of the 'I' are integrated in this fusion (which presupposes states of collective ecstasy)." For me communitas preserves individual distinctiveness—it is neither regression to infancy, nor is it emotional, nor is it "merging" in fantasy. In people's social structural relationships they are by various abstract processes generalized and segmentalized into roles, statuses, classes, cultural sexes, conventional age-divisions, ethnic affiliations, etc. In different types of social situations they have been conditioned to play specific social roles. It does not matter how well or badly as long as they "make like" they are obedient to the norm-sets that control different compartments of the complex model known as the "social structure." So far this has been almost the entire subject matter of the social sciences—people playing roles and maintaining or achieving status. Admittedly this does cover a very great deal of their available time, both in work and leisure. And, to some extent, the authentic human essence gets involved here, for every role-definition takes into account some basic human attribute or capacity, and willy-nilly, human beings *play* their roles in human ways. But *full* human capacity is locked out of these somewhat narrow, stuffy rooms. Even though when we say a person plays his role well, we often mean that he plays it with flexibility and imagination. Martin Buber's notions of *I-and-Thou* relationship and the *Essential We* formed by people moving towards a freely chosen common goal are intuitive perceptions of a non-transactional order or quality of human relationship, in the sense that people do not necessarily initiate action towards one another in the expectation of a reaction that satisfies their interests. Anthropologists, willy-nilly, have escaped many of these "hang-ups," for they deal with "man alive," in his altruistic as well as egoistic strivings, in the microprocesses of life. Some sociologists, on the other hand, find security in ethnocentric questionnaires, which, by the nature of the case, distance observer from informant, and render inauthentic their subsequently guarded interaction. In tribal societies and other pre-industrial social formations, liminality provides a propitious setting for the development of these direct, immediate, and total confrontations of human identities. In industrial societies, it is within leisure, and sometimes aided by the projections of art that this way of experiencing one's fellows can be portrayed, grasped, and sometimes realized. Liminality is, of course, an ambiguous state, for social structure, while it inhibits full social satisfaction, gives a measure of finiteness and security; liminality may be for many the acme of insecurity, the breakthrough of chaos into cosmos, of disorder into order, than the milieu of creative interhuman or transhuman satisfactions and achievements. Liminality may be the scene of disease, despair, death, suicide, the breakdown without compensatory replacement of normative, well-defined social ties and bonds. It may be *anomie,* alienation, *angst,* the three fatal *alpha* sisters of many modern myths. In tribal, etc., society it may be the interstitial domain of domestic witchcraft, the hostile dead, and the vengeful spirits of strangers; in the leisure genres of complex societies, it may be represented by the "extreme situations" beloved of existentialist writers: torture, murder, war, the verge of suicide, hospital tragedies, the point of execution, etc. Liminality is both more creative and more destructive than the structural norm. In either case it raises basic problems for social structural man, invites him to speculation and criticism. But where it is socially positive it presents, directly or by implication, a model of human society as a homogenous, unstructured communitas, whose boundaries are ideally coterminous with those of the human species. When even two people believe that they experience unity, all people are felt by those two, even if only for a flash, to be one. Feeling generalizes more readily than thought, it would seem! The great difficulty is to keep this intuition alive—regular drugging won't do it, repeated sexual union won't do it, constant immersion in great literature won't do it, initiation seclusion must sooner or later come to an end. We thus encounter the paradox that the *experience* of communitas becomes the *memory* of communitas, with the result that communitas itself in striving to replicate itself historically develops a social structure, in which initially free and innovative relationships between individuals are converted into norm-governed relationships between social *personae*. I am aware that I am stating another paradox—that the more spontaneously "equal" people become, the more distinctively "themselves" they become; the more the *same* they become socially, the less they find themselves to be individually. Yet when this communitas or *comitas* is institutionalized, the new-found idiosyncratic is legislated into yet another set of universalistic roles and statuses, whose incumbents must subordinate individuality to a rule.

As I argued in *The Ritual Process*: "The spontaneity and immediacy of communitas—as opposed to the jural-political character of (social) structure—can seldom be sustained for long. Communitas itself soon develops a (protective social) structure, in which free relationships between individuals become converted into norm-governed relationships between social personae." The so-called "normal" may be more of a game, played in masks (personae), with a script, than certain ways of behaving "without a mask," that are culturally defined as "abnormal," "aberrant," "eccentric," or "way-out." Yet communitas does not represent the erasure of structural norms from the consciousness of those participating in it; rather its own style, in a given community, might be said to depend upon the way in which it symbolizes the abrogation, negation, or inversion of the normative structure in which its participants are quotidianly involved. Indeed, its own readiness to convert into normative structure indicates its vulnerability to the structural environment.

Looking at the historical fate of communitas I identified three distinct and not necessarily sequential forms of it, which I called *spontaneous, ideological,* and *normative.* Each has certain relationships with liminal and liminoid phenomena.

(1) *Spontaneous* communitas is "a direct, immediate and total confrontation of human identities," a deep rather than intense style of personal interaction. "It has something 'magical' about it. Subjectively there is in it a

feeling of endless power.'' Is there any of us who has not known this moment when compatible people—friends, congeners—obtain a flash of lucid mutual understanding on the existential level, when they feel that all problems, not just their problems, could be resolved, whether emotional or cognitive, if only the group which is felt (in the first person) as ''essentially us'' could sustain its intersubjective illumination. This illumination may succumb to the dry light of next day's disjunction, the application of singular and personal reason to the ''glory'' of communal understanding. But when the mood, style, or ''fit'' of spontaneous communitas is upon us, we place a high value on personal honesty, openness, and lack of pretentions or pretentiousness. We feel that it is important to relate directly to another person as he presents himself in the here-and-now, to understand him in a sympathetic (not an empathetic—which implies some withholding, some non-giving of the self) way, free from the culturally defined encumbrances of his role, status, reputation, class, caste, sex or other structural niche. Individuals who interact with one another in the mode of spontaneous communitas become totally absorbed into a single synchronized, fluid event. Their ''gut'' understanding of synchronicity in these situations opens them to the understanding of such cultural forms—derived typically today from literate transmission of world culture, directly or in translation—as eucharistic union and the I Ching, which stresses the mutual mystical participation (to cite Levy-Bruhl) of all contemporary events, if one only had a mechanism to lay hold of the ''meaning'' underlying their ''coincidence.''

(2) What I have called ''*ideological* communitas'' is a set of theoretical concepts which attempt to describe the interactions of spontaneous communitas. Here the retrospective look, ''memory,'' has already distanced the individual subject from the communal or dyadic experience. Here the experiencer has already come to look to language and culture to mediate the former immediacies, an instance of what M. Csikszentmihalyi and J. MacAloon have called a ''flow-break,'' i.e., an interruption of that experience of merging action and awareness (and centering of attention) which characterized the supreme ''pay-off'' in ritual, art, sport, games and even gambling. ''Flow'' may induce communitas, and communitas ''flow,'' but some ''flows'' are solitary and some modes of communitas separate awareness from action—especially in religious communitas. Here it is not team-work in flow that is quintessential, but ''*being*'' together, with ''being'' the operative word, not ''doing.'' He has already begun to ransack the inherited cultural past for models or for cultural elements drawn from the debris of past models from which he can construct a new model which will, however falteringly, replicate in words his concrete experience of spontaneous communitas. Some of these sets of theoretical concepts can be expanded and concretized into a ''utopian'' model of society, in which all human activities would be carried out on the level of spontaneous communitas. I hasten to add that not all or even the majority of ''utopian''

models are those of "ideological communitas." Utopia means "no place" in Greek: the manufacture of utopias is an untrammelled "ludic" activity of the leisure of the modern world, and such manufacture, like industrial manufacture, tends to posit ideal politico-administrative *structures* as prime desiderata—including highly hierarchical ones—rather than what the world or land or island would look like if everyone sought to live in communitas with his and her neighbor. There are many hierarchical utopias, conservative utopias, fascistic utopias. Nevertheless, the communitas "utopia" is found in variant forms as a central ingredient, connected with the notion of "salvation," in many of the world's literate, historical religions. "Thy Kingdom" (which being caritas, agape, "love," is an anti-kingdom, a communitas) "come."

(3) *Normative* communitas, finally, is, once more, a "perduring social system," a subculture or group which attempts to foster and maintain relationships or spontaneous communitas on a more or less permanent basis. To do this it has to denature itself, for spontaneous communitas is more a matter of "grace" than "law," to use theological language. Its spirit "bloweth where it listeth"—it cannot be legislated for or normalized, since it is the *exception*, not the *law*, the *miracle*, not the *regularity*, primordial freedom, not *anangke*, the causal chain of necessity. But, nevertheless, there is something about the origin of a group based on even normative communitas which distinguishes it from groups which arise on the foundation of some "natural" or technical "necessity," real or imagined, such as a system of productive relations or a group of putatively biologically connected persons, a family, kindred, or lineage. Something of "freedom," "liberation," or "love" (to use terms common in theological or political philosophical Western vocabularies) adheres to normative communitas, even although quite often the strictest regimes devolve from what are apparently the most spontaneous experiences of communitas. This rigor comes about from the fact that communitas groups feel themselves initially to be utterly vulnerable to the institutionalized groups surrounding them. They develop protective institutional armor, armor which becomes the harder as the pressures to destroy the primary group's autonomy proportionally increase. They "become what they behold." On the other hand, if they did not "behold" their enemies, they would succumb to them. This dilemma is presumably not resolvable by a growing, changing, innovative species which invents new tools of thinking as well as of industry and explores new emotional styles as it proceeds through time. The opposition of the old may be as important for change as the innovativeness of the new, inasmuch as together they constitute a problem.

Groups based on normative communitas commonly arise during a period of religious revival. When normative communitas is demonstrably a group's dominant social mode, one can witness the process of transformation of a charismatic and personal moment into an ongoing, relatively repetitive social system. The inherent contradictions between spontaneous communitas and a markedly structured system are so great, however, that any venture with attempts to combine these modalities will constantly be threatened by structural cleavage or by the suffocation of communitas. The typical compromise here—and I refer you to *The Ritual Process,* chapter 4, for illustrative case histories—tends to be a splitting of the membership into opposed factions, a solution which endures only as long as a balance of power is maintained between them. Usually the group which first organizes, then structures itself most methodically, prevails politically or parapolitically, though the key communitas values shared by both groups but put into abeyance by the politically successful one may later become resurgent in the latter. Thus the Conventual Franciscans succeeded in getting the Spiritual Franciscans condemned for their *usus pauper,* or extreme view of poverty, but the Capuchin Reform, beginning about three centuries later in 1525, restored many of the primitive ideals of Franciscan poverty and simplicity, which were practised before the split into Conventuals and Spirituals in the 13th century. In symbological terms we have to distinguish between symbols of politico-jural systems and those making up religious systems. *Usus pauper* was a political symbol marking the factional cleavage between the two wings of Franciscanism, while "My Lady Poverty"—itself perhaps a Franciscan variant on the themes of "Our Lady Mary" or of "Our Holy Mother the Church" was a cultural symbol, transcending political structural divisions. Communitas tends to generate metaphors and symbols which later fractionate into sets and arrays of cultural values; it is in the realms of physical life-support (economics) and social control (law, politics) that symbols acquire their "social-structural" character. But, of course, the cultural and social-structural realms interpenetrate and overlap as concrete individuals pursue their interests, seek to attain their ideals, love, hate, subdue and obey one another, in the flux of history. I will not advance at this point the view that the "extended-case method," with the social drama as one of its techniques, offers a useful way of studying symbols and their meanings as events within the total flow of social events, for I am still concerned with the problem of the relationships between symbols, the liminal, the liminoid, communitas, and social structure.

Communitas exists in a kind of "figure-ground" relationship with social structure. The boundaries of each of these—in so far as they constitute explicit or implicit models for human interaction—are defined by contact or comparison with the other, just as the liminal phase of an initiation rite is defined by the surrounding social statuses (many of which it abrogates, inverts, or invalidates), and the "sacred" is defined by its relation to the "profane"—even in a single culture there is much relativity here, for if A is "sacred" to B, he may simultaneously "profane" to C, and "less sacred" to D. Situational selection prevails here, as in many other aspects of sociocultural process. Communitas, in the present context of its use, then, may be said to exist more in contrast than in active opposition to social structure, as an alternative and more "liberated" way of being socially human, a way both of being detached from social structure—and hence potentially of periodically *evaluating* its performance—and also of a "distanced" or "marginal" person's being more attached to *other* disengaged persons—and hence, sometimes of evaluating a social structure's historical performance in common with them. Here we may have a loving union of the structurally damned pronouncing judgment on normative structure and providing alternative models for structure.

Nevertheless, because the boundaries of the astructural model of human interconnectedness described by ideological communitas are "ideally coterminous with those of the human species" (and sometimes even beyond that to a generic "reverence for life"), those who are experiencing, or have recently experienced, communitas often attempt to convert a social structural interaction or a set of such interactions (involving the primacy of institutionalized status-role behavior over "freewheeling" behavior) into a direct, immediate and total confrontation of human identities, i.e., into spontaneous communitas. Communitas tends to be inclusive—some might call it "generous"—social structure tends to be exclusive, even snobbish, relishing the distinction between we/they and in-group/out-group, higher/lower, betters/menials. This drive to inclusivity makes for proselytization. One wants to make the Others, We. One famous case in the Western tradition is Pentecost, when people of different linguistic and ethnic groups claimed, under the inspiration of the Holy Ghost, to understand one another completely sub- or trans-linguistically. After that the Pentecost throng went forth to missionize the world. The glossolalia of some modern Pentecostals appears to be connected with the notion that whereas articulate speech divides people of different linguistic groups and even expedites "sin," among those of the same speech community, nonsense (archaic) speech facilitates mutual love and virtue. But these conversion attempts by communitarian individuals may be interpreted not only by the power elites of social structure, but *also* by the rank and file who feel safe in their obedience to norm, as a *direct threat* to their *own* authority or safety, and perhaps especially to their institution-based social identities. Thus the expansive tendencies of communitas may touch off a repressive campaign by the structurally entrenched elements of society, which leads in turn to more active, even militant opposition by the communitarians (cf. here the historical process set in train by many millenarian or revitalistic movements); and so on, in an ever spiralling struggle between the forces of structure and the powers of communitas—rather like what N. Frye and D. Erdman—drawing on Blake's symbols—have called the Orc-Urizen cycle—"Orc" here representing revolutionary energy and "Urizen" the "law-maker and avenging conscience" (S. Foster Damon), itself a partial anticipation of Pareto's "circulation of elites," the "lion"-like revolutionary elites succeeded by the "fox"-like strategists and tacticians of power maintenance.

In spite of—and, to a considerable extent, because of—this conflict, communitas serves important functions for the larger, structured, centristic society. In *The Ritual Process* I noted that: "Liminality, marginality, and structural inferiority are conditions in which are frequently generated myths, symbols, rituals, philosophical systems, and works of art. These cultural forms provide men with a set of templates, models, or paradigms which are, at one level, periodical reclassifications of reality (or, at least, of social experience) and man's relationship to society, nature, and culture. But they are more than (mere cognitive) classifications, since they incite men to action as well as thought."

When I wrote this, I had not yet made the distiction between ergic-ludic ritual liminality and anergic-ludic liminoid genres of action and literature. In tribal societies, liminality is often functional, in the sense of being a special duty or performance *required* in the course of work or activity; its very reversals and inversions tend to compensate for rigidities or unfairnesses of normative structure. But in industrial society, the *rite de passage* form, built into the calender and/or modelled on organic processes of maturation and decay, no longer suffices for total societies. Leisure provides the opportunity for a multiplicity of optional, liminoid genres of literature, drama, and sport, which are not conceived of as "antistructure" to normative structure where "antistructure is an auxiliary function of the larger structure" (Sutton-Smith, 1972:17). Rather they are to be seen as Sutton-Smith envisages "play," as "experimentation with variable repertoires," consistent with the manifold variation made possible by developed technology and an advanced stage of the division of labor (p. 18). The liminoid genres, to adapt Sutton-Smith (he was referring to "antistructure," a term he borrowed from me, but claimed that I used it in a system-maintenance sense only), "not only make tolerable the system as it exists, they keep its members in a more flexible state with respect to that system, and, therefore, with respect to possible change. Each system (Sutton-Smith goes on) has structural and antistructural adaptive functions. The normative structure represents the working equilibrium, the antistructure represents the latent system of potential alternatives from which novelty will arise when contingencies in the normative system require it." "We might more correctly call this second system the *protostructural* system because it is the precursor of innovative forms. It is the source of new culture" (pp. 18-19).

In the so-called "high culture" of complex societies, liminoid is not only removed from a *rite de passage* context, it is also "individualized." The solitary artist *creates* the liminoid phenomena, the collectivity *experiences* collective liminal symbols. This does not mean that the maker of liminoid symbols, ideas, images, etc., does so *ex nihilo*; it only means that he is privileged to make free with his social heritage in a way impossible to members of cultures in which the liminal is to a large extent the sacrosanct.

When we compare liminal with liminoid processes and phenomena, then, we find crucial differences as well as similarities. Let me try to set some of these out. In a crude, preliminary way they provide some delimitation of the field of comparative symbology.

(1) *Liminal phenomena* tend to predominate in tribal and early agrarian societies possessing what Durkheim has called "mechanical solidarity," and dominated by what Henry Maine has called "status." *Liminoid phenomena* flourish in societies with "organic solidarity," bonded reciprocally by "contractual" relations, and generated by and following the industrial revolution, though they perhaps begin to appear on the scene in city-states on their way to becoming empires (of the Graeco-Roman type) and in feudal societies (including not only the European sub-types found between the tenth and fourteenth centuries in France, England, Flanders, and Germany, but also in the far less "pluralistic" Japanese, Chinese, and Russian types of feudalism or quasi-feudalism). But they first begin clearly to develop in Western Europe in nascent capitalist societies, with the beginnings of industrialization and mechanization, the transformation of labor into a commodity, and the appearance of real social classes. The heyday of this type of nascent industrial society was in the seventeenth and eighteenth centuries—climaxing in the "age of enlightenment," though it had begun to appear in Western Europe in the second half of the sixteenth century, particularly in England, where, a little later, Francis Bacon published his *Novum Organum* in 1620, a work which definitely linked scientific with technical knowledge. Liminoid phenomena continue to characterize the democratic-liberal societies which dominated Europe and America in the nineteenth and early twentieth centuries, societies with universal suffrage, the predominance of legislative over executive power, parliamentarianism, a plurality of political parties, freedom of workers and employers to organize, freedom of joint stock companies, trusts, and cartels to organize, and the separation of church and state. Liminoid phenomena are still highly visible in the post-World War II managerial societies of organized capitalism of the modern U.S.A., West Germany, France, Britain, Italy, Japan, and other countries of the Western bloc. Here the economy is no longer left even ostensibly to "free competition" but is planned both by the state itself—usually in the interests of the reigning industrial and financial upper middle classes—and by private trusts and cartels (national and international), often with the support of the state, which puts its considerable bureaucratic administrative machinery in their service. Nor are liminoid phenomena absent from the systems of centralized state collectivism exemplified by Russia and China, following their revolutions, and by the "people's democracies" of Eastern Europe (with the exception of Yugoslavia, which has been moving in the direction of decentralized collectivism). Here the new culture tries to synthesize, as far as possible, humanism and technology—not the easiest of tasks—substituting for natural rhythms the logic of technological processes, while attempting to

divest these of their socially exploitative character and proposing them to be generated and sustained by the "popular genius." This, however, with collectivism, tends to reduce the potentially limitless freedom of liminoid genres to the production of forms congenial to the goal of integrating humanism (in the sense of a modern, nontheistic, rationalistic viewpoint that holds that man is capable of self-fulfillment, ethical conduct, etc., without recourse to supernaturalism) and technology.

(2) *Liminal phenomena* tend to be collective, concerned with calendrical, biological, social-structural rhythms or with crises in social processes whether these result from internal adjustments or external adaptations or remedial measures. Thus they appear at what may be called "natural breaks," natural disjunctions in the flow of natural and social processes. They are thus enforced by sociocultural "necessity," but they contain *in nuce* "freedom" and the potentiality for the formation of new ideas, symbols, models, beliefs. *Liminoid phenomena may* be collective (and when they are so, are often directly derived from liminal antecedents) but are more characteristically individual products though they often have collective or "mass" effects. They are not cyclical, but continuously generated, though in the times and places apart from work settings assigned to "leisure" activities.

(3) *Liminal phenomena* are centrally integrated into the total social process, forming with all its other aspects a complete whole, and representing its necessary negativity and subjunctivity. *Liminoid phenomena* develop apart from the central economic and political processes, along the margins, in the interfaces and interstices of central and servicing institutions—they are plural, fragmentary, and experimental in character.

(4) *Liminal phenomena* tend to confront investigators rather after the manner of Durkheim's "collective representations," symbols having a common intellectual and emotional meaning for all the members of the group. They reflect, on probing, the history of the group, i.e., its collective experience, over time. They differ from preliminal or postliminal collective representation in that they are often reversals, inversions, disguises, negations, antitheses of quotidian, "positive" or "profane" collective representations. But they share their mass, collective character.

Liminoid phenomena tend to be more idiosyncratic, quirky, to be generated by specific names individuals and in particular groups—"schools," circles, and coteries—they have to compete with one another for general recognition and are thought of at first as ludic offerings placed for sale on the "free" market—this is at least true of liminoid phenomena in nascent capitalistic and democratic-liberal societies. Their symbols are closer to the personal-psychological than to the "objective-social" typological pole.

(5) Liminal phenomena tend to be ultimately eufunctional even when seemingly "inversive" for the working of the social structure, ways of making it work without too much friction. Liminoid phenomena, on the other hand, are often parts of social critiques or even revolutionary

manifestos—books, plays, paintings, films, etc., exposing the injustices, inefficiencies, and immoralities of the mainstream economic and political structures and organizations.

In complex, modern societies both types coexist in a sort of cultural pluralism. But the liminal—found in the activities of churches, sects, and movements, in the initiation rites of clubs, fraternities, masonic orders, and other secret societies, etc.—is no longer world-wide. Nor are the liminoid phenomena which tend to be the leisure genres of art, sport, pastimes, games, etc., practised by and for particular groups, categories, segments and sectors of large-scale industrial societies of all types. But for most people the liminoid is still felt to be freer than the liminal, a matter of choice, not obligation. The *liminoid* is more like a commodity—indeed, often *is* a commodity, which one selects and pays for—than the *liminal,* which elicits loyalty and is bound up with one's membership or desired membership in some highly corporate group. One *works* at the liminal, one *plays* with the liminoid. There may be much moral pressure to go to church or synagogue, whereas one queues up at the box office to see a play by Beckett, a show of Mort Sahl's, a Super-bowl Game, a symphony concert, or an art exhibition. And if one plays golf, goes yachting, or climbs mountains, one often needs to buy expensive equipment or pay for club membership. Of course, there are also all kinds of "free" liminoid entertainments and performances—Mardi Gras, charivari, home entertainments of various kinds—but these already have something of the stamp of the liminal upon them, quite often they are the cultural debris of some forgotten liminal ritual. There are permanent "liminoid" settings and spaces, too—bars, pubs, some cafes, social clubs, etc. But when clubs become exclusivist they tend to generate rites of passage, with the *liminal* a condition of entrance into the *liminoid* realm.

I am frankly in the exploratory phase just now. I hope to make more precise these crude, almost medieval maps I have been unrolling of the obscure liminal and liminoid regions which lie around our comfortable village of the sociologically known, proven, tried and tested. Both "liminal" and "liminoid" mean studying symbols in social action, in praxis, not entirely at a safe remove from the full human condition. It means studying all domains of expressive culture, not the high culture alone nor the popular culture alone, the literate or the non-literate, the Great or the Little Tradition, the urban or the rural. Comparative symbology must learn how to "embrace multitudes" and generate sound intellectual progeny from that embrace. It must study *total* social phenomena.

I would like to conclude by considering some of the relationships between communitas, "flow," the liminal, and liminoid. Let me briefly try to explain what Csikszentmihalyi and MacAloon mean by "flowing." "Flow denotes the holistic sensation present when we act with total involvement," and is "a state in which action follows action according to an internal logic which seems to need no conscious intervention on our part . . . we experience it as a unified flowing from one moment to the next, in which we feel in control of our actions, and in which there is little distinction between self and environment; between stimulus and response; or between past, present, and future'' (''Play and Intrinsic Rewards,'' unpublished mss.). Some recent research by Callois, Unsworth, Abrahams, Murphy (and by MacAloon and Csikszentmihalyi) has focused on various forms of play and sport (liminoid metagenres of our society) such as mountaineering, rock-climbing, soccer, hockey, chess, long-distance swimming, handball, etc., in which the state of flow can be experienced. Csikszentmihalyi extends the notion of ''flow'' beyond play to ''creative experience'' in art and literature, and to religious experiences, drawing on many scientific and literary sources. He locates six ''elements'' or ''qualities'' or ''distinctive features'' of the ''flow experience.'' These are:

(1) *The experience of merging action and awareness:* there is no dualism in ''flow''; while an actor may be aware of what he is doing, he cannot be aware that he is aware—if he does, there is a rhythmic behavioral or cognitive break. Self-consciousness makes him stumble. ''Flow'' perceived from the ''outside'' becomes non-''flow'' or anti-''flow.'' Pleasure gives way to problem, to worry, to anxiety.

(2) This merging of action and awareness is made possible by a *centering of attention* on a limited stimulus field. Consciousness must be narrowed, intensified, beamed in on a limited focus of attention. ''Past and future must be given up''—only *now* matters. How is this to be done? Here the conditions that normally prevail must be ''simplified'' by some definition of situational relevance. What is irrelevant must be excluded. Physiological ways of doing this are drugs and alcohol, which do not so much ''expand'' consciousness as limit and intensify awareness. Intensification is the name of the game. In games this is done by formal *rules* and by such *motivational* means as competitiveness. A game's rules dismiss as irrelevant most of the ''noise''which makes up social reality,the multiform stimuli which impinge on our consciousness. We have to abide by a limited set of norms. Then we are motivated to *do well* by the game's intrinsic structure, often to *do better* than others who subscribe to the same rules. Our minds and our will are thus disencumbered from irrelevances and sharply focused in certain known directions. *Rewards* for good knowledge and invincible will, when harnessed to tactical technical skill, complete the focusing. But for our authors, ''the flow's the thing,'' not the rules, motivations, or rewards. This involves ''inner resources'' too, the ''will to participate'' (which like all liminoid phenomena goes back to voluntariness; one *opts* to play), the capacity to shift emphases among the structural components of a game, or to innovate by using the rules to generate unprecedented performances. But it is the limitation by rules and motive, the centering of attention, which en-

courages the flow experience.

(3) *Loss of ego* is another "flow" attribute. The "self" which is normally the "broker" between one person's actions and another's, simply becomes irrelevant—the actor is immersed in the "flow," he accepts the rules as binding which are also binding on the other actors—no self is needed to "bargain" about what should or should not be done. The rules ensure the reduction of deviance or eccentricity in much of manifest behavior. Reality tends to be "simplified to the point that is understandable, definable, and manageable" (p. 11). This holds good, Csikszentmihalyi says, for "religious ritual, artistic performance, games." Self-forgetfulness here does not mean loss of self-awareness. Kinesthetic and mental awareness is indeed heightened, not reduced—but its full effect is broken, as we have seen; the special kind of awareness of self intrinsic to it is lost. Again, there is no solipsism, mere autism, about the experience. Flow reaches out to nature and to other men in what Csikszentmihalyi calls "intuitions of unity, solidarity, repletion and acceptance." All men, even all things, are felt to be one, subjectively, in the flow experience—and much data is brought forward to support this. Levy-Bruhl's "participation mystique" and Suzuki's "non-dualistic (Zen) experience" are cited as well as the comments of athletes and sportsmen.

(4) A person "in flow" finds himself *"in control of his actions and of the environment."* He may not know this at the time of "flow," but reflecting on it he may realize that his skills were matched to the demands made on him by ritual, art, or sport. This helps him to "build a positive self-concept" (p. 13). Outside "flow," such a subjective sense of control is difficult to attain, due to the multiplicity of stimuli and cultural tasks—especially, I would hold, in industrial societies, with their complex social and technical division of labor. But in the ritualized limits of a game or the writing of a poem, a man or woman may *cope,* if they rise to the occasion with skill and tact. With control, worry and fear goes. Even, as in rock-climbing, when the dangers are real, the moment "flow" begins and the activity is entered, the flow "delights" outweigh the sense of dangers and problems.

(5) "Flow" usually contains coherent, *non-contradictory demands for action,* and provides *clear, unambiguous feedback* to a person's actions. This is entailed by the limiting of awareness to a restricted field of possibilities. Culture reduces the flow possibility to defined channels—chess, polo, gambling, liturgical action, miniature painting, a yoga exercise, etc. You can "throw yourself" into the cultural design of the game or art, and know whether you have done well or not when you have finished the round of culturally predetermined acts—in the extreme case, if you survive, you have performed adequately. In other cases, the public or the critics have an important say, but if you are a real "pro," the final judge is yourself, looking back. Flow differs from everyday in that it contains explicit rules "which make action and the evaluation of action unproblematic" (p. 15). Thus, cheating

breaks flow—you have to be a believer, even if this means temporary "willing suspension of disbelief," i.e., choosing (in liminoid fashion) to believe that the rules are "true."

(6) Finally "flow" is "autotelic," i.e., *it seems to need no goals or rewards outside itself.* To flow is to be as happy as a human can be—the particular rules or stimuli that triggered the flow, whether chess or a prayer meeting, do not matter. This is important for any study of human behavior, if true, for it suggests that people will culturally manufacture situations which will release flow, or individually seek it outside their ascribed stations in life if these are "flow-resistant."

Csikszentmihalyi goes on to link "flow theory" with information theory and competence theory, but I am not convinced by these speculations. I think he has superbly pinpointed and ascribed qualities to this experience—which *has* to be dealt with phenomenologically in the first place (though we may be able to get more "objective" later with EEG patterns, changes in metabolic rate, etc.).

I would like to say simply that what I call *communitas* has something of a "flow" quality, but it may arise, and often does arise spontaneously and unanticipated—it does not need rules to trigger it off. In theological language, it is sometimes a matter of "grace" rather than "law." Again, "flow" is experienced within an individual, whereas communitas at its inception is evidently between or among individuals—it is what all of us believe we share and its outputs emerge from dialogue, using both words and non-verbal means of communication, such as understanding smiles, jerks of the head, and so on, between us. "Flow" for me is already in the domain of what I have called "structure," communitas is always prestructural, even though those who participate in it have been saturated in structure—being human—since they were infants. But "flow" for me seems to be one of the ways in which "structure" may be transformed or "liquefied" (like the famed martyr's blood) into communitas again. It is one of the techniques whereby people seek the lost "kingdom" or "anti-kingdom" of direct, unmediated communion with one another, even though severe subscription to rules is the frame in which communion may possibly be induced (the "mantric" frame, one might say).

In societies before the Industrial Revolution, ritual could always have a "flow" quality for total communities (tribes, moieties, clans, lineages, families, etc.); in post-industrial societies, when ritual gave way to individualism and rationalism, the flow experience was pushed mainly into the leisure genres of art, sport, games, pastimes, etc. Since work was complex and diversified, its pleasurable, optational equivalent, palliative, or medicine, the domain of leisure genres, also became complex and diversified. However, it was often inversive of the work domain in form if not in function—since the function of many games is to reinforce the mental paradigms we all carry in our heads which motivate us to carry out energetically the tasks our culture defines as belonging to the "work" sphere.

The point here is that ritual (including its liminal phase) in archaic, theocratico-charismatic, patriarchal, and feudal societies (even a little in city-states becoming empires) and certain ancillary institutions such as religious drama provided the main cultural flow-mechanisms and patterns. But in those ages in which the sphere of religious ritual has contracted (as Durkheim puts it), a multiplicity of (theoretically) non-serious, non-earnest genres, such as art and sport (though these may be more serious than the Protestant ethic has defined them to be), have largely taken over the flow-function in culture. Communitas is something else, for it does not have to be induced by rules—it can happen anywhere, often in despite of rules. It is more like the "Witness" in Hindu thought which can only watch and love, but *cannot* act (i.e., cannot "flow" in games terms) without changing its nature.

One final point: I have left out both from communitas and "flow" an essential feature—the *content* of the experience. This is where the analysis of symbols begins—the symbols of chess, of Impressionist art, of Buddhist meditation, of Christian Marian pilgrimage, of scientific research, of formal logic, have different meanings, different semantic contents. Surely, the processes of communitas and flow are imbued with the meanings of the symbols they either generate or are channelled by. Are all "flows" one and do the symbols indicated different kinds and depths of flow?

References

Abrahams, Roger, and Richard Bauman. "Ranges of Festival Behavior." Paper presented to Symposium on "Forms of Symbolic Inversion." American Anthropological Association, Toronto, December 1, 1972.

Barthes, Roland. *Elements of Semiology*. London: Jonathan Cape, 1967.

Beal, Samuel. *Travels of Fah-Hian and Sung-Yun*. London: Susil Gupta, 1964. First published 1869.

Csikszentmihalyi, Mihaly. *Flow: Studies of Enjoyment*. University of Chicago, PHS Grant Report, 1974.

—. "Play and Intrinsic Rewards," *Journal of Humanistic Psychology, 1975. Page references from unpublished manuscript, 1972.*

—. *Beyond Boredom and Anxiety: The Experience of Play in Work and Games*. San Francisco: Jossey-Bass, 1975.

Danielou, Alain. *Hindu Polytheism*. New York: Bollinger Foundation, 1964.

Dumazedier, Joffre. *Le Loisir et la ville*. Paris: Editions du Seuil, 1962.

—. Article on "Leisure," in David Sills, ed., *Encyclopedia of the Social Sciences*. New York: Macmillan and Free Press, pp. 248-253, 1968.

Gennep, Arnold van. *The Rites of Passage*. London: Routledge and Kegan Paul, 1960. First published 1909.

Grazia, Sebastian de. *Of Time, Work, and Leisure*. New York: Twentieth Century Fund, 1962.

Gurvitch, Georges. "Mass, Community, Communion." *Journal of Philosophy*. August, 1941.

Nikhilananda, Swami. *The Bhagavad Gita*. New York: Ramakrishna-Vivekananda Center, 1969.

Norbeck, Edward. "Man at Play," in *Play, a Natural History Magazine Supplement*, pp. 48-53, December, 1971.

Piaget, Jean. *Play, Dream, and Imitation*. New York: Norton, 1962.

Singer, Milton. *When a Great Tradition Modernizes*. New York: Praeger, 1972.

Sutton-Smith, Brian. "Games of Order and Disorder." Paper presented to Symposium on "Forms of Symbolic Inversion." American Anthropological Association, Toronto, December 1, 1972.

Turner, Victor. *Schism and Continuity*. Manchester: Manchester University Press, 1957.

—. *The Forest of Symbols*. Ithaca: Cornell University Press, 1967.

—. *The Ritual Process*. Chicago: Aldine, 1969.

—. *Dramas, Fields, and Metaphors*. Ithaca: Cornell University Press, 1974.

Watson, William. "Social Mobility and Social Class in Industrial Communities," in Max Gluckman, ed., *Closed Systems and Open Minds*. Edinburgh: Oliver and Boyd, 1965.

Social Dramas
and
Stories About Them

Anthropologists count and measure what they can in order to establish general features of the sociocultural fields they study. Although these activities have their irritating side, on the whole I found it eminently soothing, during my two and a half years of fieldwork among the Ndembu of northwestern Zambia, a West-Central Bantu-speaking people, to sit in villages before a calabash of millet or honey beer and collect numerical data on village membership, divorce frequency, bridewealth, labor migration rates, individual cash budgets, birth and homicide rates, and more strenuously to measure the acreage of gardens and dimensions of ritual enclosures. In a way these figures told me, if not a story, at least where to go to find stories. For I was able to infer from statistics based on censuses and genealogies of some seventy villages that these residential units consisted of cores of closely related male matrilineal kin, their wives and children, and sisters who as a result of frequent divorce had returned to their natal villages bringing their junior children with them. This was, of course, only the thin end of a massive wedge. I soon discovered that Ndembu married *virilocally*, that is, a woman goes after marriage to reside in her husband's village. Consequently, in the long run, village continuity depends upon marital discontinuity, since one's right to reside in a given village is primarily determined by matrilineal affiliation, though one may reside in one's father's village during his lifetime. Clearly a sort of structural turbulence is "built in" to these normative arrangements. For a village can only persist by recruiting widows, divorcees, and their children. There is also a propensity for men, who reside in their own matrilineal village, to persuade their sisters to leave their husbands, bringing with them the children who "properly belong" to that village. Political authority, chieftainship, headmanship, and other offices are in male hands, even in this matrilineal society: however, a man cannot be succeeded by his own son, but by his uterine brother or his sister's son. The chain of authority, therefore, demands that, sooner or later, a headman's sister's sons will leave their paternal villages and dwell with their maternal uncle. It is easier to do this if a young man is residing with his stepfather, not the father "who begat him." Thus divorce works in various ways to reassert the ultimate paramountcy of the maternal line, despite the masculine attempt to preempt the present through virilocal marriage. It is far from my mind to insist on the mysteries of anthropological terminology with the spiky cacophonies of its neologisms, no spikier, it may be said, than those of other academic tribes, but it is pertinent to my discussion of the varied valencies of narrative, to show how certain entrenched features of a given society's social structure influence both the course of conduct in observable social events and the scenarios of its genres of cultural performance—ranging from ritual to *märchen*. To complete the simplified picture of Ndembu social structure I should mention, however, that in several books (1957, 1967, 1968, 1969) I have tried to work out how stresses between matrilineal succession, and other principles and the processes to which they give rise, have affected various mundane and ritual phenomena, processes, and institutions of Ndembu society, such as village size, composition, mobility, fissiveness, marital stability, relations between and within genealogical generations, the role of the many situationally invoked cult associations in counterbalancing cleavages in villages, lineages and families, the strong masculine stress on complex hunting and circumcision rites in a system ultimately dependent on women's agricultural and food-processing activities, and the patterning of witchcraft accusations—which are often directed against matrilineal rivals for office or prestige.

I suppose that if I had confined myself to the analysis of numerical data, guided by knowledge of salient kinship principles and political, legal and economic contexts, I would have construed an anthropological narrative informed by what Hayden White (1973:16) in his book *Metahistory* surely would have called "mechanistic" presuppositions. Indeed, this was standard practice in the British School of structuralist-functionalist anthropology in which I was nurtured in the late forties and early fifties. One of its main aims was to exhibit the laws of structure and process which, in a given preliterate society, determine the specific configurations of relationships and institutions detectable by trained observation. The ultimate intent of this school, as formulated by Radcliffe-Brown, was by the comparative method to seek out general laws by successive approximation. Each specific ethnography sought for general principles that appeared in the study of a single society. In other words, idiographic procedures, detailed descriptions of what I actually observed or learned from informants, were pressed into the service of the development of laws. Hypotheses developed out of idiographic research were tested nomothetically, i.e., for the purpose of formulating general sociological laws.

There are, of course, many virtues in this approach. My figures *did* give me some measure of the relative importance of the principles on which Ndembu villages are socially constructed. They pointed to trends in the direction of individual and corporate spatial mobility. They indicated how in some areas particularly exposed to the modern cash economy, a smaller type of residential unit based on the polygynous family, called a "farm," was replacing the traditional circular village whose nucleus was a sibling group of matrilineal kin. The method I used was also employed by colleagues working from the Rhodes-Livingstone Institute and facilitated controlled comparison of village structures belonging to different Central African societies. Differences of kinship and local structures were compared with differences in such variables as the divorce rate, the amount of bridewealth, the mode of subsistence, and so forth.

Nevertheless, this approach has its limitations. As George Spindler (1978:31) has argued, "the idiography of ethnography may be distorted by the nomethetic orientation of the ethnographer." In other words, the general theory you take into the field leads you to select certain data for attention, but blinds you to others perhaps more important for the understanding of the people studied. As I came to know Ndembu well both in stressful and uneventful times as "men and women alive" (to paraphrase D.H. Lawrence), I become increasingly aware of this limitation. Long before I had read a word of Wilhelm Dilthey's I had shared his notion that "structures of experience" are fundamental units in the study of human action. Such structures are irrefrangibly threefold, being at once cognitive, conative, and affective. Each of these terms is itself, of course, a shorthand for a range of processes and capacities. Perhaps this view was influenced by Edward Sapir's celebrated essay in the *Journal of Social Psychology* (1934, 5:410-16), "Emergence of a Concept of Personality in a Study of Culture," in which he wrote: "In spite of the oft-asserted impersonality of culture, a humble truth remains that vast reaches of culture, far from being 'carried' by a group or community . . . are discovered only as the peculiar property of certain individuals, who cannot but give these cultural goods the impress of their own personality" (p. 412). Not only that, but persons will desire and feel as well as think, and their desires and feelings impregnate their thoughts and influence their intentions. Sapir assailed cultural overdeterminism as a reified cognitive construct of the anthropologist, whose "impersonalized" culture is hardly more than "an assembly of loosely overlapping ideas and action systems, which, through verbal habit, can be made to assume the appearance of a closed system of behavior" (p. 411), a position corresponding to some extent with Hayden White's organicist paradigm—as prestigious among American anthropologists as functionalism was among their British contemporaries. It became clear to me that an "anthropology of experience" would have to take into account the psychological properties of individuals as well as the culture which, as Sapir insists, is *"never given"* to each individual, but, rather, "gropingly discovered," and, I would add, some parts of it quite late in life. We never cease to learn our *own* culture, let alone other cultures, and our own culture is always changing. It also became clear that among the many tasks of the anthropologist lay the duty not only to make structuralist and functionalist analyses of statistical and textual data (censuses and myths), but also to prehend experiential structures in the actual processes of social life. Here my own approach, and that of many other anthropologists, conforms to some extent with White's contextualist model. White, using Pepper's term, sees contextualism as the isolation of some element of the historical field (or, in the anthropological instance, the sociocultural field) as the subject of study, "whether the element be as large as the French Revolution or as small as one day in the life of a specific person. The investigator then proceeds to pick out the 'threads' that link the event to be explained to different areas of the context. The threads are identified and traced outward, into the circumambient natural and social space in which the event occurred, and both backward in time, in order to determine the 'origins' of the event, and forward in time, in order to determine its 'impact' and 'influence' on subsequent events. This tracing operation ends at the point at which the 'threads' either disappear into the 'context' of some other 'event' or 'converge' to cause the occurrence of some new 'event.' The impulse is not to integrate *all* the events and trends that might be identified in the whole historical field, but rather to link them together in a chain of provisional and restricted characterizations of finite provinces of manifestly 'significant' occurrence" (pp. 18-19). It is interesting to pause here for a moment and compare how Sapir and White use the metaphor of "thread." For Sapir points out (op. cit., 411) that the "purely formalized and logically developed schemes" we call ethnographies do not explain behavior until "the *threads* [my emphasis] of symbolism and implication that connect patterns or parts of patterns with others, of an entirely different formal aspect" are discovered. For Sapir these "threads" are *internal* to the sociocultural space studied, and relate to the personality and temperament of individuals, while for White and Pepper, "threads" describe the nature of connections between an "element" or "event" and its significant *environing* sociocultural field viewed, according to White, "synchronically" or "structurally" (p. 19). I find fascinating Sapir's notion that his "threads" are *"symbolic"* and *"implicative"*; for symbols, the spawn of such tropes as arise in the interaction of men and women alive, metaphors, synechdoches, metonymies new minted in crises, so to speak, really do come to serve as semiotic connectives among the levels and parts of a system of action and between that system and its significant environment. We have been neglecting the role of symbols in establishing connexity between the different levels of a narrative structure.

But I am anticipating. I shall shortly call attention to a kind or species of "element of the historical field" or "event," in White's terminology, which is cross-culturally isolable and which exhibits, if it is allowed to come to full term, a characteristic processual structure, a structure that holds firm whether one is considering a macro- or micro-historical event of this type. Before I discuss this unit, which I consider to be the social ground of many types of "narrative," and which I have called "social drama," I must first mention for the benefit of my non-anthropologist readers another useful distinction made by anthropologists, that between "emic" and "etic" perspectives, these terms being derived from the distinction made by linguists between *phonemic* and *phonetic*, the former being the study of sounds recognized as distinct *within* a specific language, the latter being the cross-lingual study of distinguishable human sound units. Kenneth Pike, who propounded this dichotomy, should be allowed to formulate it: "Descriptions of analyses from the etic standpoint are 'alien,' with criteria external to the system. Emic descriptions provide an internal view (or an 'inside view' in Hockett's terms), with criteria chosen from within the system. They represent to us the view of one familiar with this system and who knows how to function within it himself" (1954:8). From this standpoint all four of the strategies of explanation proposed by White drawing on Stephen Pepper—formism, organicism, mechanism, and contextualism—would produce "etic" narratives, if they were used to provide accounts of societies outside that Western cultural tradition generatively triangulated by the thinking of Jerusalem, Athens, and Rome, and continued in the philosophical, literary, and social-scientific traditions of Europe, North America, and their cultural offshoots. Indeed, members of such societies (the so-called "Third World") have protested (for example, the Ethiopian anthropologist, Asmarom Legesse, in *Gada*, 1973:283), that Western attempts to "explain" their cultures amount to no more than "cognitive ethnocentrism," diminishing their contribution to the global human reflexivity which modern communicational and informational systems are now making possible, if hardly easy. In other words, what we in the West consider "etic," that is, "nomothetic," "non-culture-bound," "scientific," "objective," they are coming to regard as "emic," the mental product of a portion of world-culture whose bearers could say, rather smugly, until very recently, with Thomas Hardy, but without a trace of his ironical intent, that "We have got the Gatling Gun, and they have not."

There are then *both* etic and emic ways of regarding narrative. An anthropologist, embedded in the life of an at-first-wholly-other culture and separated, save in memory, from his own, has to come to terms with that which invests and invades him. The situation is odd enough. He is tossed into the ongoing life of a parcel of people who not only speak a different language but also classify what we would call "social reality" in ways that are at first quite unexpected. He is compelled to learn, however haltingly, the criteria which provide the "inside view."

I am aware of Hayden White's "theory of the historical work,"and that bears importantly upon how to write ethnographies as well as histories, but I am also aware that any discussion of the role of narrative in other cultures requires that an emic description of narrative be made. For the anthropologist's work is deeply involved in what *we* might call "tales," "stories," "folk-tales," "histories," "gossip," and "informants' accounts," types of narrative for which there may be many native names, not all of which coincide with our terms. Indeed, Max Gluckman has commented that the very term "anthropologist" means in Greek "one who talks about men," in other words, a "gossip." In our culture we have many ways of talking about men, descriptive and analytical, formal and informal, traditional and open-ended. Since ours is a literate culture, characterized by a refined division of cultural labor, we have devised numerous specialized genres by means of which we scan, describe, and interpret our behavior towards one another. But the impulse to talk about one another in different ways, in terms of different qualities and levels of mutual consciousness, precedes literacy in all human communities. All human acts and institutions are developed, as Clifford Geertz might say, in webs of interpretive words. Also, of course, we mime and dance one another—we have webs of interpretive nonverbal symbols. And we play one another—beginning as children, and continuing through life to learn new roles and the subcultures of higher statuses to which we aspire, partly seriously, partly ironically.

Ndembu make a distinction, akin to White's division between "chronicle" and "story" as levels of conceptualization in Western culture, between *nsang'u* and *kaheka*. *Nsang'u* may refer, for example, to a purportedly factual record of the migration of the Lunda chiefs and their followers from the Katanga region of Zaire on the Nkalanyi River, their encounter with the autochthonous Mbwela or Lukolwe peoples in Mwinilunga District, battles and marriages between Lunda and Mbwela, the establishment of Ndembu-Lunda chiefdoms, the order of chiefly incumbents down to the present (the praise-names and praise-songs for chiefs themselves amounting to a kind of chronicle), the raids of Luvale and Tchokwe in the nineteenth century to secure indentured labor for the Portuguese in San Tome long after the formal abolition of the slave trade, the coming of the missionaries, followed by the British South Africa Company, and finally British Colonial rule. *Nsang'u* may also denote an autobiographical account, a personal reminiscence, or an eye-witness report of yesterday's interesting happening. *Nsang'u*, like "chronicle," in White's words (*op.cit.*:

5) arranges "the events to be dealt with in the temporal order of their occurrence." Just as a chronicle becomes a "story," in White's usage, "by the further arrangement of the events into components of a 'spectacle' or process of happening, which is thought to possess a discernible beginning, middle, and end . . . in terms of inaugural motifs . . . transitional motifs . . . and terminal motifs," so does *nsang'u* become *kaheka*, chronicle becomes story. This term covers a range of tales which our folklorists would no doubt sort out into a number of "etic" types: myth, folktale, *märchen*, legend, ballad, folk epic, and the like. Their distinctive feature is that they are part told, part sung. At key points in the narration the audience joins in a sung refrain, breaking the spoken sequence. It depends on the context of situation and the mode of framing whether a given set of events is regarded as *nsang'u* or *kaheka*. Take, for example, the series of tales about the ancient Lunda chief Yala Mwaku, his daughter Lweji Ankonde, her lover the Luban hunter-prince Chibinda Ilung'a, and her brothers Ching'uli and Chinyama (I use the Southern Lunda pronunciation of these names), their loves, hates, conflicts and reconciliations, which led, on the one hand, to the establishment of the Lunda nation, and, on the other, to the secession and diaspora of dissident Lunda groups, thereby spreading knowledge of centralized political organization over a wide territory. This sequence may be told by a chief of putative Lunda origin in his court to politically influential visitors as an *nsang'u*, a "chronicle," perhaps to justify his title to his office. But episodes from this chronicle may be transformed into *tuheka* (plural of *kaheka*), "stories," and told by old women to groups of children huddled near the kitchen fire during the cold season. A particular favorite, analyzed recently by the distinguished Belgian structuralist Luc de Heusch in *Le Roi Ivre*, relates how the drunken king Yala Mwaku was derided and beaten by his sons, but cared for tenderly by his daughter Lweji Ankonde, whom he rewarded by passing on to her, on his death, the royal bracelet, the *lukanu* (made of human genitalia for the magical maintenance of the fertility of humans, animals, and crops in the whole kingdom), thus rendering her the legitimate monarch of the Lunda. Another tells of how the young queen is told by her maidens that a handsome young hunter, having slain a waterbuck, had camped with his companions on the far side of the Nkalanye River. She summons him to her presence and the two fall in love at once and talk for many hours in a grove of trees (where today a sacred fire, the center of an extensive pilgrimage, burns constantly). She learns that he is the youngest son of a great Luba chief, but that he prefers the free life of a forest hunter to the court. Nevertheless, from love he marries Lweji, and, in time, receives from her the *lukanu*—she has to go into seclusion during menstruation and hands Chibinda the bracelet lest it become polluted—making him the ruler of the Lunda nation. Southern Lunda folk etymology even derives the term "Lunda" from the noun *Wulunda*, "love" or "close friendship." Lweji's turbulent brothers refuse to recognize him, and lead their people away to carve out new kingdoms for themselves and

consequently spread the format of political centralization among stateless societies. Jan Vansina, the noted Belgian ethnohistorian, has discussed the relationship between this foundation narrative and the political structures of the many Central African societies who claim that they "came from Mwantiyanvwa," as the new dynasty came to call itself, in his book, *Kingdoms of the Savanna* (1966). He finds in this corpus of stories more than myth, although de Heusch has illuminatingly treated it as such; Vansina finds clues to historical affinities between the scattered societies who assert Lunda origin; indications corroborated by other types of evidence, linguistic, archaeological, and cultural. As in other cultures, the same events may be framed as *nsang'u* or *kaheka*, chronicle or story, often according to their nodal location in the life-process of the group or community that recounts them. It all depends where and when and by whom they are told. Thus, for some purposes the foundation tales of Yala Mwaku and Lweji are treated as chronicle, to advance a political claim, for example, to "Lundahood," as Ian Cunnison calls their assertion of descent from prestigious migrants. For the purpose of entertainment, in the village men's shelter in the evening or women's kitchens, the same tales are defined as "stories," with many rhetorical touches and flourishes as well as songs inserted as evocative embellishment. Incidents may even be cited during processes of litigation to legitimate or reinforce the claims of a plaintiff in a dispute over boundaries or succession to office.

For the anthropologist, however, who is concerned with the study of social action and social process, it is not these formal genres of tale-telling and tale-bearing that most grip his attention, but rather, as we have seen, what we would call "gossip," talk and rumors about the private affairs of others, what the Ndembu and their neighbors, the Luvale, call *kudiyongola*, related to the verb *kuyong'a*, "to crowd together," for much gossip takes place in the central, unwalled shelter of traditional villages, where the circumcised, hence socially "mature," males foregather, to discuss community affairs, and hear the "news" (*nsang'u*) of other communities from wayfarers. The critic Frank Kermode once defined the novel as consisting of two components: scandal and myth. Certainly gossip (which includes scandal) is one of the perennial sources of cultural genres. Gossip does not occur in a vacuum among the Ndembu; it is almost always "plugged in" to the unit of social process that I briefly described in the Introduction—the social drama.

Although it might be argued that the social drama is a "story" in Hayden White's sense, in that it has discernible inaugural, transitional, and terminal motifs, cultural markers that it has a beginning, a middle, and an end, my observations convince me that it is, indeed, a spontaneous unit of social process and a fact of everyone's experience in every human society. My hypothesis, based on repeated observations of such processual units in a range of socio-cultural systems, and on my reading in ethnography and history, is that social dramas, "dramas of living," as Kenneth Burke calls them, can be aptly studied as having four phases. These I label: breach, crisis, redress, and *either* reintegration *or* recognition of schism. Social dramas occur within groups bounded by shared values and interests of persons and having a real or alleged common history. Their main actors are persons for whom the group which constitutes the field of dramatic action has a high value priority. Most of us have what I like to call our "star" group or groups to which we owe our deepest loyalty and whose fate is for us of the greatest personal concern. We are all members of many groups, formal or informal, from the family to the nation or some international religious or political institution. Each person makes his/her own subjective evaluation of their respective worth: some are "dear" to one, others it is one's "duty to defend," and so on. Some tragic situations arise from conflicts of loyalty to different "star" groups. A star group is the one with which a person identifies most deeply and in which he finds fulfillment of his major social and personal strivings and desires. There is no *objective* rank order in any culture for such groups. I have known academic colleagues whose supreme star group, believe it or not, was a particular faculty administrative committee, and whose families and recreational groups ranked much lower, others whose love and loyalty were towards the local Philatelic Society. In every culture one is *obliged* to belong to certain groups, usually institutionalized ones—family, age-set, school, firm, professional association, and the like. But such groups are not necessarily one's beloved chosen star groups. It is in one's star group that one looks most for love, recognition, prestige, office, and other tangible and intangible benefits and rewards. In it one achieves self-respect and a sense of belonging with others for whom one has respect. Now every objective group has members some of whom see it as their star group, while others may regard it with indifference, even dislike. Relations among the "star-groupers," as the first category may be called, are often highly ambivalent, resembling those among members of an elementary family for which, perhaps, the star group is an adult substitute. They recognize one another's common attachment to the group, but are jealous of one another over the relative intensity of that attachment or the esteem in which another member is held by the group as a whole. They may contend with each other for the incumbency of high office in the group, not merely to seek power but out of the conviction that they, and they alone, really understand the nature and value of the group and can altruistically advance its interests. In other words, we find symbolic equivalents of sibling rivalry and parent-child competition among "star-groupers."

In several books (1957, 1967, 1968, 1974) I have discussed social dramas at some length, both in small-scale societies, such as Ndembu, at the village level, and on the scale of complex nations, as in the power struggle between Henry II of England and Archbishop Thomas Becket and the Hidalgo Insurrection in early nineteenth century Mexico. Whether it is large affair, like the Dreyfuss Case or Watergate, or a struggle for village headmanship, a social drama first manifests itself as the breach of a norm, the infraction of a rule of morality, law, custom or etiquette in some public arena. This breach may be deliberately, even calculatedly, contrived by a person or party disposed to demonstrate orchallenge entrenched authority—for example, the Boston Tea Party—or it may emerge from a scene of heated feelings. Once visible, it can hardly be revoked. Whatever the case, a mounting crisis follows, a momentous juncture or turning point in the relations between components of a social field—at which seeming peace becomes overt conflict and covert antagonisms become visible. Sides are taken, factions are formed, and unless the conflict can be sealed off quickly within a limited area of social interaction, there is a tendency for the breach to widen and spread until it coincides with some dominant cleavage in the widest set of relevant social relations to which the parties in conflict belong. We have seen this process at work in the Iranian crisis following the breach precipitated by the seizure of the U.S. Embassy in Teheran. The phase of crisis exposes the pattern of current factional struggle within the relevant social group, be it village or world community; and beneath it there becomes slowly visible the less plastic, more durable, but nevertheless gradually changing basic social structure, made up of relations which are relatively constant and consistent. For example, I found that among the Ndembu, prolonged social dramas always revealed the related sets of oppositions that give Ndembu social structure its tensile character: matriliny versus virilocality; the ambitious individual versus the wider interlinking of matrilineal kin; the elementary family versus the uterine sibling group (children of one mother); the forwardness of youth versus the domineering elders; status-seeking versus responsibility; sorcerism (*wuloji*)—that is, hostile feelings, grudges, and intrigues—versus friendly respect and generosity towards others. In the Iranian crisis we saw the emergence to public visibility of divisions and coalitions of interests, some of which are surprising and revelatory. Love may be "a many splendored thing," but crisis is certainly a "many-levelled thing" in all cultures. In social dramas, false friendship is winnowed from true communality of interests; the limits of consensus are reached and realized; real power emerges from behind the facade of authority.

In order to limit the contagious spread of *breach* certain adjustive and redressive mechanisms, informal and formal, are brought into operation by leading members of the disturbed group. These mechanisms vary in character with such factors as the depth and significance of the breach, the social inclusiveness of the crisis, the nature of the social group within which the breach took place, and its degree of autonomy in regard to wider systems of social relations. The mechanisms may range from personal advice and informal arbitration, to formal juridical and legal machinery, and to resolve certain kinds of crisis, to the performance of public ritual. Such ritual involves a "sacrifice," literal or moral, a victim as scapegoat for the group's "sin" of redressive violence.

The final phase consists either in the reintegration of the disturbed social group—though, as like as not, the scope and range of its relational field will have altered; the number of its parts will be different; and their size and influence will have changed—or the social recognition of irreparable breach between the contesting parties, sometimes leading to their spatial separation. This may be on the scale of the many Exoduses of history or merely a move of disgruntled villagers to a spot a few miles away. This phase, too, may be registered by a public ceremony or ritual, indicating reconciliation or permanent cleavage between the parties involved.

I am well aware that the social drama is an agonistic model drawn after a recurrent agonistic situation, and I make no claim that there are no other types of processual unit. Gulliver, for example, studying another Central African society, the Ndendeuli of Tanzania, directs attention to the cumulative effect of an endless series of minor incidents, cases, and events that might be quite as significant in affecting and changing social relationships as the more overtly dramatic encounters. Raymond Firth discusses "harmonic" processual units—which I call "social enterprises" that also have recognizable phase structure. These stress "the process of ordering of action and of relations in reference to given social ends" and are often economic in type. Quite often, though, such "enterprises"—as in the case of urban renewal in America—become social dramas, if there is resistance to the aims of their instigators. The resisters perceive the inauguration of the enterprise as "breach," not "progress." Nor does the course of a social drama—like "true love"—always "run smooth." Redressive procedures may break down, with reversion to crisis. Traditional machinery of conciliation or coercion may prove inadequate to cope with new types of issues and problems, and new roles and statuses. And, of course, reconcilation may only seem to have been achieved in phase four, with real conflicts glossed over but not resolved. Moreover, at certain historical junctures in large-scale complex societies, redress may be through rebellion, or even revolution, if the societal value-consensus has broken down, and new unprecedented roles, relationships, and classes have emerged.

Nevertheless, I would persist in arguing that the social drama is a well-nigh universal processual form, and represents a perpetual challenge to all aspirations to perfection in social and political organization. In some cultures its profile is clear-cut and style abrasive: in others, agonistic (contestative) action may be muted or deflected by elaborate codes of etiquette. In yet others conflict may be—to cite Richard Antoun on Arab village politics in Jordan—"low-key," eschewing direct confrontation and encounter in its style. Social dramas are in large measure political processes, that is, they involve competition for scarce ends—power, dignity, prestige, honor, purity—by particular means and by the utilization of resources that are also scarce—goods, territory, money, men and women. Ends, means, and resources are caught up in an interdependent feedback process. Some kinds of resources, for example, land, money, may be converted into others, for instance, honor and prestige (which are simultaneously the needs sought). Or they may be employed to stigmatize rivals and deny them these ends. According to my observations, the political aspect of social dramas is dominated by those I have called "star-groupers." They are the main protagonists, the leaders of factions, the defenders of the faith, the revolutionary vanguard, the arch-reformers. These are the ones who develop to an art the rhetoric of persuasion and influence, who know how and when to apply pressure and force, and are most sensitive to the factors of legitimacy. In Phase Three, redress, it is the "star-groupers" who manipulate the machinery of redress, the law-courts, the procedures of divination and ritual, and impose sanctions on those adjudged to have precipitated crisis, just as it may well be disgruntled or dissident star-groupers who lead rebellions and provoke the initial breach.

The fact that a social drama, as I have analyzed its form, closely corresponds to Aristotle's description of tragedy in the *Poetics*, in that it is "the imitation of an action that is complete, and whole, and of a certain magnitude . . . having a beginning, a middle, and an end," is not, I repeat, because I have tried inappropriately to impose an "etic" Western model of stage action upon the conduct of an African village society, but because there is an interdependent, perhaps dialectic, relationship between social dramas and genres of cultural performance in perhaps all societies. Life, after all, is as much an imitation of art as the reverse. Those who, as children in Ndembu society, have listened to innumerable stories about Yala Mwaku and Luweji Ankonde, know all about "inaugural motifs"—"when the king was drunk and helpless, his sons beat and reviled him"—"transitional" motifs—"his daughter found him near death and comforted and tended him"—and "terminal" motifs—"the king gave his daughter the *lukanu* and excluded his sons from the royal succession." When these same Ndembu, now full-grown, wish to provoke a breach or to claim that some party has crucially disturbed the placid social order, they have a frame available to "inaugurate" a social drama, with a repertoire of "transitional" and "ending" motifs to continue the framing process and channel the subsequent agonistic developments. Just as the story itself still makes important points about family relationships and about the stresses between sex- and age-roles, and appears to be an emic generalization, clothed in metaphor and involving the projection of innumerable specific social dramas generated by these structural tensions, so does it feed back into the social process, providing it with a rhetoric, a mode of employment, and a meaning. Some genres, particularly epic, serve as paradigms which inform the action of important political leaders—star-groupers of encompassing groups such as Church or State—giving them style, direction, and sometimes compelling them subliminally to follow in major public crisis a certain course of action, thus emplotting their lives. I tried to show in *Dramas, Fields, and Metaphors* (1975: chapter 2) how Thomas Becket, after his antagonistic confrontation with both Henry II and the bench of Bishops at the Council of Northampton, seemed to have been almost "taken over," "possessed" by the action-paradigm provided by the *Via Crucis* in Christian belief and ritual, sealing his love-hate relationship with Henry in the conjoined image of martyr and martyrizer—and giving rise to a subsequent host of narratives and aesthetic dramas. By paradigm I do not mean a system of univocal concepts, logically arrayed. I do not mean either a stereotyped set of guidelines for ethical, aesthetic, or conventional action. A paradigm of this sort goes beyond the cognitive and even the moral to the existential domain; and in so doing becomes clothed with allusiveness, implications, and metaphor—for in the stress of action, firm definitional outlines become blurred by the encounter of emotionally charged wills. Paradigms of this type, cultural root paradigms, so to speak, reach down to irreducible life stances of individuals, passing beneath conscious prehension to a fiduciary hold on what they sense to be axiomatic values, matters literally of life and death. Richard Schechner (1977) has sought to express the relationship between social drama and aesthetic or staged drama in the form of a figure eight placed in a horizontal position and then bisected through both loops:

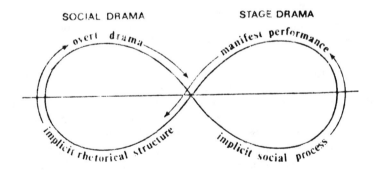

The left loop represents the social drama; above the line is the overt drama, below it, the implicit rhetòrical structure; the right loop represents stage drama; above the line is the manifest performance, below it, the implicit social process, with its structural contradictions. Arrows pointing from left to right represent the course of action. They follow the phases of the social drama above the line in the left loop, descending to cross into the lower half of the right loop where they represent the hidden social in-frastructures. The arrows then ascend and, moving now from right to left, pass through the successive phases of a generalized stage drama. At the point of intersection between the two loops, they descend once more to form the hidden aesthetic model underpinning, so to speak, the overt social drama. This model, though effective, is somewhat equilibrist in its implications for my taste, and suggests cyclical rather than linear movement. But it has the merit of pointing up the dynamical relation between social drama and expressive cultural genres. The social drama of Watergate was full of "*stage* business" during every phase, from the Guy Fawkes-like con-spiratorial atmosphere of the "breach" episode, signalized by the finding of the incriminating tape of the door, through the tough minded fictionality of the cover-up, and all that went into the "crisis" phase of investigation, with its Deep Throat revelations and combinations of high-minded princi-ple and low-minded political opportunism. The redressive phase was no less implicitly scripted by theatrical and fictional models. I need not describe the Hearings and the Saturday Night Massacre. Now we have plays, films, and novels about Watergate and its *dramatis personae naturalis*, which are shaped—to use the aseptic language of social science—in accord with the structure and properties of the social field environing and penetrating their authors at the time of writing. At the deepest level we may anticipate an interpretive shift towards accommodation of the most accep-table texts to some deeply entrenched paradigm of Americanity. The American "myth," as Sacvan Bercovitch has argued in his book *The American Jeremiad* (1978), periodically produces "jeremiads" (polemical homilies in various cultural genres) against declension into ways of life which reek of the static, corrupt, hierarchical Old World, and obviate movement towards an ever receding but ultimately reachable promised land to be craved from some unsullied wilderness, where an ideal, pro-sperous democracy can thrive "under God." Watergate is a superb target for the American jeremiad. Paradoxically, many of its personages have become celebrities, but this may not be so surprising after all. Pontius Pilate was canonized by the Ethiopean Church, and if Dean and Ehrlichman will never perhaps be seen as saints, their mere participation in a drama which activated a major cultural paradigm has conferred on them an ambiguous eminence they might otherwise have never achieved. The winners of social dramas positively require cultural performances to con-tinue to legitimate their success. And such dramas generate their "symbolic types" (R. Grathoff, 1970; Don Handelman, 1979): traitors, renegades, villains, martyrs, heroes, faithful, infidels, deceivers, scapegoats. Just to be in the cast of a narrated drama which comes to be taken as exemplary or paradigmatic is some assurance of social immortality.

It is the third phase of a social drama, redress, that has most to do with the genesis and sustentation of cultural genres, both "high" and "folk," oral and literate. In *Schism and Continuity*, I argued that in Ndembu society when conflict emerges from the opposed interests and claims of protagonists acting under a single social principle, say, descent from a common ancestress, judicial institutions can be invoked to meet the crisis, for a rational attempt can be made to adjust claims that are similarly based. But when claims are advanced under different social principles, which are inconsistent with one another even to the point of mutual contradiction, there can be no rational settlement. Here Ndembu have recourse to divination of sorcery or ancestral wrath to account for misfortune, illness, or death occurring before or during the social drama. Ultimately, rituals of reconciliation may be performed, which, in their verbal and nonverbal symbolism, reassert and reanimate the overarching values shared by all Ndembu, despite conflicts of norms and interests on ground level.

Whether juridical or ritual processes of redress are invoked against mounting crisis, the result is an increase in what one might call social or plural *reflexivity*, the ways in which a group tries to scrutinize, portray, understand, and then act on itself. Barbara Myerhoff has written of cultural performances ("Life History Among the Elderly: Performance, Visibility, and Remembering," n.d., p. 5) that they are *"reflective* in the sense of showing ourselves to ourselves. They are also capable of being *reflexive*, arousing consciousness of ourselves as we see ourselves. As heroes in our own dramas, we are made self aware, conscious of our consciousness. At once actor and audience, we may then come into the fullness of our human capability—and perhaps human desire to watch ourselves and enjoy knowing that we know." I tend to regard the social drama in its full formal development, its full phase structure, as a process of converting particular values and ends, distributed over a range of actors, into a system (which is always temporary and provisional) of shared or consensual meaning. It has not yet reached the stage of Myerhoff's enjoying that we know that we know ourselves, but it is a step in that direction. I am inclined to agree with Wilhelm Dilthey (see H. Hodges, 1952:272-3) that *meaning* (*Bedeutung*) arises in *memory*, in *cognition* of the *past*, and is concerned with negotiation about the "fit" between past and present, whereas *value* (*Wert*) inheres in the affective enjoyment of the *present*, while the category of *end* (*Zweck*) or *good* (*Gut*) arises from *volition*, the power or faculty of using the will, which refers to the *future*. The redressive phase, in which feedback on crisis is provided by the scanning devices of law (secular ritual) and religious ritual, is a liminal time, set apart from the ongoing business of quotidian life, when an interpretation (*Bedeutung*) is constructed to give the appearance of sense and order to the events leading up to and constituting the crisis. It is only the category of meaning, so Dilthey tells us, that enables us to conceive of an intrinsic affinity between the successive events of life, or, one might add, of a social drama. In the redressive phase the meaning of the social life informs the apprehension of itself, while the object to be apprehended enters into and reshapes the apprehending subject. Pure anthropological functionalism, whose aim is to state the conditions of social equilibrium among the components of a social system at a given time, cannot deal with meaning, for meaning always involves retrospection and reflexivity, a past, a history. Meaning is the only category which grasps the full relation of the part to the whole in life, for value, being dominantly affective, belongs essentially to an experience in a conscious present. Such conscious presents, regarded purely as present moments, totally involve the experiencer, even to the extent that they have no intrinsic connection with one another, at least of a systematic, cognitive kind. They stand behind one another in temporal sequence, and, while they may be compared as "values," that is, as having the same epistemological status, they do not form anything like a coherent whole, for they are essentially momentary, transient, insofar as they are values alone; if they are interconnected, the ligatures that bind them belong to another category—that of *meaning*, relexivity arrived at. In stage drama, values would be the province of actors, meaning that of the producer. Values exist in what Csikszentmihalyi would call the state of "flow." Reflexivity tends to inhibit flow, for it articulates experience. Dilthey eloquently hits off the unarticulated quality of value: "From the standpoint of value, life appears as an infinite assortment of positive and negative existence-values. It is like a chaos of harmonies and discords. Each of these is a tone-structure which fills a present; but they have *no musical relation* to one another" [my emphasis]. To establish such a musical relation, the liminal reflexivity of the redressive phase is necessary if crisis is to be rendered meaningful. Crises are "like a chaos of harmonies and discords." Some modern modalities of music, I think, try to replicate this chaos, let it stand as it is—for the meaning-ligatures inherited from the past no longer bind. Here we must return to narrative.

For both the legal and ritual procedures generate *narratives* from the brute facts, the mere empirical coexistence of experiences, and endeavor to lay hold of the factors making for integration in a given situation. Meaning is apprehended by *looking back* over a temporal process: it is generated in the "narrative" constructed by lawmen and judges in the process of cross-examination from witnesses' evidence, or by diviners from their intuitions into the responses of their clients as framed by their specific hermeneutic techniques. The meaning of every part of the process is assessed by its contribution to the total result.

It will be noted that my basic social drama is agonistic, rife with problem and conflict, and this is not merely because it assumes that sociocultural systems are never logical systems or harmonious *gestalten*, but are fraught with structural contradictions and norm-conflicts. The true opposition should not be defined in these "objectivized" terms. It is between indeterminacy and all modes of determination. Indeterminacy is, so to speak, in the "subjunctive mood," since it is that which is not yet settled, concluded, and known. It is all that may be, might be, could be, perhaps even should be. It is that which terrifies in the breach and crisis phases of a social drama. Sally Falk Moore goes so far as to suggest that "the underlying quality of social life should be considered to be one of theoretical absolute indeterminacy" (1978:48). Social reality is "fluid and indeterminate," though, for her, "regularizing processes" and "processes of situational adjustment," represent human aspirations constantly to transform it into organized or systematic forms. But even where ordering rules and customs are strongly sanctioned, "indeterminacy may be produced and ambiguities within the universe of relatively determinate elements." Such manipulation is characteristic of breach and crisis. It may also help to resolve crisis. The third phase, redress, reveals that "determining" and "fixing" are indeed processes, not permanent states or givens. They proceed by assigning meanings to events and relationships in reflexive narratives. Indeterminacy should not be regarded as the absence of social being; it is not negation, emptiness, privation. Rather it is potentiality, the possibility of becoming. From this point of view social being is finitude, limitation, constraint. Actually it only "exists" as a set of cognitive models in actors' heads or as more or less coherent "objectivized" doctrines and protocols. Ritual and legal procedures mediate between the formed and the indeterminate. As Moore argues, "ritual is a declaration of form against indeterminacy, *therefore* indeterminacy is always present in the background of any analysis of ritual." In 1979 I attended several sessions of the *Umbanda* religion at a cult center (*terreiro*) in Rio de Janeiro and found that the medium-possessing *Orixa* or Entity known as *Exu,* of West African Yoruba origin, where he is the Trickster deity of the Crossroads, in several ways personifies this "meonic" (to use Nicholas Berdyaev's term) indeterminacy. He is sometimes represented on Umbanist altars as a being (*Entitade*) with two heads: one face is that of Christ, the other, Satan's. *Exu,* whose ritual colors are black and red, is the Lord of the Limen and of Chaos, the full ambiguity of the subjunctive mood of culture, representing the indeterminacy that lurks in the cracks and crevices of all socio-cultural "constructions of reality," the one who must be kept at bay if the framed formal order of the ritual proceedings is to go forward according to protocol. He is the abyss of possibility; hence his two heads, for he is both potential savior and tempter. He is also destroyer, for in one of his modes he is Lord of the Cemetery. Like Shiva, Creator and Destroyer, he wields a trident. One may see his image and sign in New York and Montreal, if one scans carefully the costumes (known as "fantasies") of the Caribbean *Mardi Gras* carnivals—for he is worshipped in Cuban and Puerto Rican *Santeria* religion, as well as in Brazilian *Candomble* and *Umbanda.* In all major cultural process, from ritual to theatre and the novel, of any complexity of meaning, there are both "sequence and secrets"—to quote Kermode again—"secrets" are those non-sequential bits of creative indeterminacy which get into, and apparently seem to foul up all coherent protocols, scripts, texts, whatsoever little hints of the abyss of subjunctivity, that break in and out like *Exu* and threaten the measured movement towards climax on cultural terms.

The social drama, then, I regard as the experiential matrix from which the many genres of cultural performance, beginning with redressive ritual and juridical procedures, and eventually including oral and literary narrative, have been generated. Breach, crisis, and reintegrative or divisive outcomes provide the content of such later genres, redressive procedures their form. As society complexifies, as the division of labor produces more and more specialized and professionalized modalities of sociocultural action, so do the modes of assigning meaning to social dramas multiply—but the drama remains to the last simple and ineradicable, a fact of everyone's social experience, and a significant node in the developmental cycle of all groups that aspire to continuance. The social drama remains humankind's thorny problem, its undying worm, its Achilles' heel—one can only use cliches for such an obvious and familiar pattern of sequentiality. At the same time it is our native way of manifesting ourselves to ourselves and, of declaring where power and meaning lie and how they are distributed.

In *The Ritual Process* and in these essays, I have discussed van Gennep's discovery of the processual form of the *rite de passage*, and will refer to it again shortly. Rites of passage, like social dramas, involve temporal processes and agonistic relations—novices or initiands are separated (sometimes real or symbolic force is used (from a previous social state or status, compelled to remain in seclusion during the liminal phase, submitted to ordeal by initiated seniors or elders, and re-aggregated to quotidian society in symbolic ways that often show that preritual ties have been irremediably broken and new relationships rendered compulsory. But, like other kinds of rituals, life-crisis rituals, the most transformative kind of rites of passage, already exhibit a marked degree of generalization—they are the fairly late product of social reflexivity. They confer on the actors, by nonverbal as well as verbal means, the experiential understanding that social life is a series of movements in space and time, a series of changes of activity, and a series of transitions in status for individuals. They also inscribe in them the knowledge that such movements, changes, and transitions are not merely marked but also effected by ritual. Ritual and juridical procedures represent germinative components of social drama, from which, I suggest, many performative and narrative modes of complex culture derive. Cultural performances may be viewed as "dialectical dancing partners" (to use Ronald Grimes's phrase) of the perennial social drama, to which they give meaning appropriate to the specificities of time, place, and culture. However, they have their own autonomy and momentum; one genre may generate another; with sufficient evidence in certain cultural traditions one might be able to reconstruct a reasonably accurate genealogy of genres. (I use advisedly these terms derived from the Indo-European root *gan*, "to beget or produce," as metaphors for their ready cultural reproductiveness.) Or one genre might supplant or replace another as the historically or situationally dominant form "social metacommentary" (to use Geertz's illuminating term). New communicative techniques and media may make possible wholly unprecedented genres of cultural performance, making possible new modes of self-understanding. Once a genre has become prominent, however, it is likely to survive or be revived at some level of the sociocultural system, perhaps moving from the elite to the popular culture or vice-versa, gaining and losing audiences and support in the process. Nevertheless, all the genres have to circle, as it were, around the earth of the social drama, and some, like satellites, may exert tidal effects on its inner structure. Since ritual in the so-called "simpler" societies is so complex and many-layered it may not unfittingly be considered an important "source" of later (in cultural evolutionary terms), more specialized, performative genres. Often when ritual perishes as a dominant genre, it dies, a *multipara*, giving birth to ritualized progeny, including the many performative arts.

In earlier publications I defined "ritual" as "prescribed formal behavior for occasions not given over to technological routine, having reference to beliefs in invisible beings or powers regarded as the first and final causes of all effects"—a definition which owes much to those of Auguste Comte, Godfrey and Monica Wilson, and Ruth Benedict. I still find this formulation operationally useful despite Sir Edmund Leach, and other anthropologists of his ilk, who would eliminate the religious component and regard ritual as "stereotyped behavior which is potent in itself in terms of the cultural conventions of the actors, though not potent in a rational-technical sense," and which serves to communicate information about a culture's most cherished values. I find it useful, because I like to think of ritual essentially as *performance, enactment*, not primarily as rules or rubrics. The rules "frame" the ritual process, but the ritual process transcends its frame. A river needs banks or it will be a dangerous flood, but banks without a river epitomize aridity. The term "performance" is, of course, derived from Old English *parfournir*, literally "to furnish completely or thoroughly." To perform is thus to bring something about, to consummate something, or to "*carry out*" a play, order, or project. But in the "carrying out," I hold, something new may be generated. The performance transforms itself. True, as I said, the rules may "frame" the performance, but the "flow" of action and interaction within that frame may conduce to hitherto unprecedented insights and even generate new symbols and meanings, which may be incorporated into subsequent performances. Traditional framings may have to be reframed—new bottles made for new wine. It is here that I find the notion of orientation to preternatural and invisible beings and powers singularly apposite. For there is undoubtable transformative capacity in a well-performed ritual, implying an ingress of power into the initial situation; and "performing well" implies the co-involvement of the majority of its performers in a self-transcending flow of ritual events. The power may be drawn from the persons of the drama, but drawn from their human depths, not entirely from their cognitive, "indicative" hold on cultural skills. Even if a rubrical book exists prescribing the order and character of the performance of the rites, this should be seen as a source of channelings, rather than of dictates. The experience of subjective and inter-subjective flow in ritual performance, whatever its sociobiological or personalogical concomitants may be, often convinces performers that the ritual situation *is* indeed informed with powers both transcendental and immanent. Moreover, most anthropological definitions of ritual, including my own earlier attempts, have failed to take into account van Gennep's discovery that rituals nearly always "accompany transitions from one situation to another and from one cosmic or social world to another" (*Les Rites de Passage,* p. 13). As is well known he divides these rituals into rites of separation, threshold rites, and rites of re-aggregation, for which he also employs the terms preliminal, liminal, and postliminal. The order in which the ritual events follow one another and must be performed, van Gennep points out, is a religious element of essential importance. To exist at all, writes Nicole Belmont about van Gennep's notion, "a ritual must first and foremost be inscribed in time and space, or rather reinscribed" if it follows a prior model given in myth (*Arnold Van Gennep: The Creator of Fench Ethnography,* 1979:64). In other words, performative *sequencing* is intrinsic and should be taken into account in any definition of ritual. Here I would query the formal structuralist implication that sequence is an illusion and all is but a permutation and combination of rules and vocabularies already laid down in the deep structures of mind and brain. There *is* a qualitative distinction between successive stages in social dramas and rites of passage which renders them irreversible—their sequence is no illusion—the unidirectional movement is transformative. I have written at some length about the "threshold" or liminal phase of ritual, and found it fruitful to extend the notion of liminality as metaphor to other domains of expressive cultural action than ritual. But liminality must be taken into account in any serious formulation of ritual as performance, for it is in connection with this phase that "emic" folk characterizations of ritual lay strongest stress on the transformative action of "invisible or supernatural beings or powers regarded as the first and final causes of all effects." Without taking liminality into account ritual becomes indistinguishable from "ceremony," "formality," or what Barbara Myerhoff and Sally Moore, in their Introduction to *Secular Ritual* (1977) indeed call "*secular* ritual." The liminal phase is the essential, *anti*-secular component in ritual *per se*, whether it be labeled "religious" or "magical." Ceremony *indicates*, ritual *transforms*, and transformation occurs most radically in the ritual "pupation" of liminal seclusion—at least in life-crisis rituals. The public liminality of great seasonal feasts exhibits its fantasies and "transforms" (akin here to the linguistic sense of "transform," that is, [a] any of a set of rules for producing grammatical transformations of a kernel sentence; [b] a sentence produced by using such a role) to the eyes of all—and so does postmodern theatre—but that is a matter for a different paper.

I have also argued that ritual in its performative plenitude in tribal and many post-tribal cultures is a matrix from which several other genres of cultural performance, including most of those we tend to think of as "aesthetic" have been derived. It is a late modern Western myth, encouraged perhaps by depth psychologists, and, lately by ethnologists, that ritual has the rigid precision characteristics of the "ritualized" behavior of an obsessive neurotic, or a territory-marking animal or bird, and also encouraged by an early modern Puritan myth that ritual is "mere empty form without true religious content." It is true that rituals may become mere shells or husks at certain historical junctures, but this state of affairs belongs to the senescence or pathology of the ritual process, not to its "normal working." Living ritual may be better likened to artwork than neurosis. Ritual is, in its most typical cross-cultural expressions, a synchronization of many performative genres, and is often ordered by *dramatic* structure, a plot, frequently involving an act of sacrifice or self-sacrifice, which energizes and gives emotional coloring to the interdependent communicative codes which express in manifold ways the meaning inherent in the dramatic *leitmotiv*. In so far as it is "dramatic," ritual contains a distanced and generalized reduplication of the agonistic process of the social drama. Ritual, therefore, is not "threadbare" but "richly textured" by virtue of its varied interweavings of the productions of mind and senses. Participants in the major rituals of vital religions, whether tribal or post-tribal, may be passive and active in turn with regard to the ritual movement, which as van Gennep, and, more recently, Roland Delattre, have shown, draws on biological, climatic, and ecological rhythms, as well as on social rhythms, as models for the processual forms it sequentially employs in its episodic structure. *All* the senses of participants and performers may be engaged; they *hear* music and prayers, *see* visual symbols, *taste* consecrated foods, *smell* incense, and *touch* sacred persons and objects. They also have available the kinesthetic forms of dance and gesture, and perhaps cultural repertoires of facial expression, to bring them into significant performative rapport. Here I should mention in this connection Judith Lynne Hanna's useful book *To Dance is Human: A Theory of Nonverbal Communication* (1979) in which she attempts to construct a sociocultural theory of dance. In song, participants merge (and diverge) in other ordered and symbolic ways. Moreover, few rituals are so completely stereotyped that every word, every gesture, every scene is authoritatively prescribed. Most often, invariant phases and episodes are interdigitated with variable passages, in which, both at the verbal and nonverbal levels, improvisation may not be merely permitted but required. Like the black and white keys of a piano, like the *Yin* and *Yang* interplay in Chinese religious cosmology and Taoist ritual, constancy and mutability make up, in their contrariety, a total instrument for the expression of human meaning, joyous, sorrowful, and both at once, "woven fine," in William Blake's words. Ritual, in fact, far from being merely formal, or formulaic, is a symphony in more than music. It can be—and often is—a symphony or synaesthestic ensemble of expressive cultural genres, or, a synergy of varied symbolic operations, an opus which unlike "opera" (also a multiplicity of genres as Wagner repeatedly emphasized) escapes opera's theatricality, though never life's inexpugnable social drama, by virtue of the seriousness of its ultimate concerns. The "flat" view of ritual must go. So also must the notion, beloved until recently by functionalist anthropologists, that ritual could be best understood as a set of mechanism for promoting a gross group solidarity, as, in fact, a "sort of all-purpose social glue," as Robin Horton characterized this position, and that its symbols were merely "reflections or expressions of components of social structure." Ritual, in its full performative flow, is not only many-leveled, "laminated," but also capable, under conditions of societal change, of creative modification on all or any of its levels. Since it is tacitly held to communicate the deepest values of the group regularly performing it, it has a *"paradigmatic"* function, in both of the senses argued for by Clifford Geertz. As a *"model for"* ritual can anticipate, even generate change; as a *"model of,"* it may inscribe order in the minds, hearts, and wills of participants.

Ritual, in other words, is not only complex and many-layered; it has an *abyss* in it, and indeed, is an effort to make meaningful the dialectical relation of what the Silesian mystic Jakob Boehme, following Meister Eckhart, called "Ground" and "Underground," "Byss and Abyss" (= the Greek *a-bussos*, ʼἂβυσσος, from a-"without," and the Ionic variant of the Attic *buthos*, βύθοs , meaning "bottom," or, better, [finite] "depth," especially "of the sea." So "byss" is deep but "abyss" is beyond all depth.) Many definitions of ritual contain the notion of *depth*, but few of *infinite* depth. In the terminology I favor, such definitions are concerned with finite structural depth, not with infinite "antistructural" depth. A homelier analogy, drawn from linguistics, would be to say that the passage form of ritual, as elicited by van Gennep, postulates a unidirectional move from the *"indicative"* mood of cultural process, through culture's *"subjunctive"* mood back to the *"indicative"* mood, though this recovered mood has now been tempered, even transformed, by immersion in subjunctivity; this process roughly corresponds with his preliminal, liminal, and postliminal phases. In preliminal rites of separation the initiand is moved from the indicative quotidian social structure into the subjunctive antistructure of the liminal process and is then returned, transformed by liminal experiences, by the rites of reaggregation to social structural participation in the indicative mood. The subjunctive, according to Webster's Dictionary, is always concerned with "wish, desire, possibility, or hypothesis"; it is a world of "as if," ranging from scientific hypothesis to festive fantasy. It is "if it *were* so," not "it *is* so." The indicative prevails in the world of what in the West we call "actual fact," though this definition can range from a close scientific inquiry into how a situation, event, or agent produces an effect or result, to a lay person's description of the characteristics of ordinary good sense or sound practical judgment. Sally Moore and Barbara Myerhoff, in their introduction to *Secular Ritual*, did not use this pair of terms, "subjunctive" and "indicative," but, rather, saw social process as moving "between the formed and the indeterminate" (p. 17). They are, however, mostly discussing "ceremony" or "secular ritual," not ritual *pur sang*. I agree with them, as I said earlier, that "all collective ceremony can be interpreted as a cultural statement about cultural order as against a cultural void" (p. 16), and that "ceremony is a declaration against indeterminacy. Through form and formality it celebrates man-made meaning, the culturally determinate, the regulated, the named, and the explained. It banishes from consideration the basic questions raised by the made-upness of culture, its malleability and alternability . . . [every ceremony] seeks to state that the cosmos and social world, or some particular small part of them are orderly and explicable and for the moment fixed. A ceremony can allude to such propositions and demonstrate them at the same time . . . Ritual [*sic*, really "ceremony"] is a declaration of form *against* [Moore and Myerhoff's emphasis] indeterminacy, therefore indeterminacy is always present in the background of any analysis of ritual" (pp. 16-17). Roy Rappaport in his book, *Ecology, Meaning, and Religion* (1979:206), adopts a similar standpoint when he writes: "Liturgical orders [whose "sequential dimension," he says, is ritual] bind together disparate entities and processes, and it is this binding together, rather than what is bound together that is peculiar to them. Liturgical orders are meta-orders, or orders of orders . . . they mend ever again worlds forever breaking apart under the blows of usage and the slashing distinctions of language."

While I consider these to be admirably lucid statements about ceremony, which, for me, constitutes an impressive institutionalized performance of indicative, normatively structured social reality, and is also both a model *of* and a model *for* social states and statuses, I do not think such formulations can be applied with equal cogency to ritual. For ritual, as I have said, does not portray a dualistic, almost Manichean, struggle between order and void, cosmos and chaos, formed and indeterminate, with the former always triumphing in the end. Rather is it a transformative self-immolation of order as presently constituted, even sometimes a voluntary *sparagmos* or self-dismemberment of order, in the subjunctive depths of liminality. One thinks of Eliade's studies of the "shaman's journey" where the initiand is broken into pieces then put together again as a being bridging visible and invisible worlds. Only in this way, through destruction and reconstruction, that is, transformation, may an authentic reordering come about. Actuality takes the sacrificial plunge into possibility and emerges as a different kind of actuality. We are not here in the presence of two like but opposed forces as in Manichean myth; rather there is a qualitative incongruence between the contraries engaged, though Jung's daring metaphor of the incestuous marriage of the conscious ego with the unconscious seen as an archetypal mother, poses that relationship in terms of paradoxical kinship and affinity. Subjunctivity is fittingly the mother of indicativity, since any actualization is only one among a myriad possibilities of being, some of which may be actualized in space-time somewhere or somewhen else. The "hard saying" "except ye become as a little child" assumes new meaning. Unless the fixing and ordering processes of the adult, *sociostructural* domain, are liminally abandoned and the initiand submits to being broken down to a generalized *prima materia,* a lump of human clay, he cannot be transformed, reshaped to encounter new experiences.

Ritual's liminal phase, then, approximates to the "subjunctive mood" of sociocultural action. It is, quintessentially, a time and place lodged between all times and spaces defined and governed in any specific biocultural ecosystem (A. Vayda, J. Bennett, and the like) by the rules of law, politics and religion, and by economic necessity. Here the cognitive schemata that give sense and order to everyday life no longer apply, but are, as it were, suspended—in ritual symbolism perhaps even shown as destroyed or dissolved. Gods and goddesses of destruction are adored primarily because they personify an essential phase in an irreversible transformative process. All further growth requires the immolation of that which was fundamental to an earlier stage—"lest one good custom should corrupt the world." Clearly, the liminal space-time "pod" created by ritual action, or today by certain kinds of reflexively ritualized theatre, is potentially perilous. For it may be opened up to energies of the biopsychical human constitution normally channeled by socialization into status-role activities, to employ the unwieldy jargon of the social sciences. Nevertheless, the danger of the liminal phase conceded, and respected by hedging it around by ritual interdictions and taboos, it is also held in most cultures to be regenerative, as I mentioned earlier. For in liminality what is mundanely bound in sociostructural form may be unbound and rebound. Of course, if a society is in hairline-precarious subsistence balance with its environment, we are unlikely to find in its liminal zones very much in the way of experimentation—here one does not fool around with the tried and tested. But when a "biocultural ecosystem," to use Vayda's terms, produce significant surpluses, even if these are merely the seasonal boons of a naturally well-endowed environment, the liminality of its major rituals may well generate cultural surpluses too. One thinks of the Kwakiutl and other Northwest

Amerindian peoples with their complex iconographies and formerly rich hunting and gathering resources. New meanings and symbols may be introduced—or new ways of portraying or embellishing old models for living, and so of renewing interest in them. Ritual liminality, therefore, contains the potentiality for cultural innovation, as well as the means of effecting structural transformations within a relatively stable sociocultural system. For many transformations are, of course, within the limits of social structure, and have to do with its internal adjustments and external adaptations to environmental changes. Cognitive structuralism can cope best with such relatively cyclical and repetitive societies.

In tribal and agrarian cultures, even relatively complex ones, the innovative potential of ritual liminality seems to have been circumscribed, even dormant, or pressed into the service of maintaining the existing social order. Even so, room for "play," Huizinga's *ludic*, abounds in many kinds of tribal rituals, even in funerary rituals. There is a play of *symbol*-vehicles, leading to the construction of bizarre masks and costumes from elements of mundane life now conjoined in fantastic ways. There is a play of *meanings*, involving the reversal of hierarchical orderings of values and social statuses. There is a play with *words* resulting in the generation of secret initiatory languages, as well as joyful or serious punning. Even the dramatic scenarios which give many rituals their processual armature may be presented as comedic rather than serious or tragic. Riddling and joking may take place, even in the liminal seclusion of initiatory lodges. Recent studies of Pueblo ritual clowns recall to us how widespread the clown role is in tribal and archaic religious culture. Liminality is peculiarly conducive to play, where it is not restricted to games and jokes, but extends to the introduction of new forms of symbolic action, such as word-games or original masks.

But whatever happened to liminality, as societies increased in scale and complexity, particularly Western industrial societies? With deliminalization seems to have gone the powerful *play* component. Other religions of the Book, too, have tended regularly to stress the solemn at the expense of the festive. Religiously connected fairs, fiestas and carnivals do continue to exist, of course, but not as intrinsic parts of liturgical systems. The great Oriental religions—Hinduism, Taoism, Tantric Buddhism, Shintoism, however, still recognize in many public performances that human ritual can be both earnest *and* playful. Eros may sport with Thanatos, not as a grisly Danse Macabre, but to symbolize a complete human reality and a Nature full of oddities.

It would seem that with industrialization, urbanization, spreading literacy, labor migration, specialization, professionalization, bureaucracy, the division of the leisure sphere from the work sphere by the firm's clock, the former integrity of the orchestrated religious *gestalt* that once constituted ritual has burst open and many specialized performative genres have been born from the death of that mighty *opus deorum hominumque.* These genres of industrial leisure would include theatre, ballet, opera, film, the novel, printed poetry, the art exhibition, classical music, rock music, carnivals, processions, folk drama, major sports events and dozens more. Disintegration has been accompanied by secularization. Traditional religions, their rituals denuded of much of their former symbolic wealth and meaning, hence their transformative capacity, persist in the leisure sphere, but have not adapted well to modernity. Modernity means the exaltation of the indicative mood—but in what Ihab Hassan has called the "postmodern turn," we may be seeing a re-turn to subjunctivity and a rediscovery of cultural transformative modes, particularly in some forms of theatre. Dismembering may be a prelude to re-membering. Re-membering is not merely the restoration of some past intact, but setting it in living relationship to the present.

However, there are signs that those nations and cultures which came late to the industrial table, such as Japan, India, the Middle Eastern nations, and much of South and Central America, have succeeded, at least in part, in avoiding the dismemberment of important ritual types, and they have incorporated into their ritual performances many of the issues and problems of modern urban living and succeeded in giving them religious meaning. When industrial development came to much of the Third World it had to confront powerfully consolidated structures of ritual performative genres. In the West similar institutions had been gradually eroded from within, from the revival of learning to the Industrial Revolution. Here the indicative mood triumphed, and subjunctivity was relegated to a reduced domain where admittedly it shone brighter in the arts than in religion.

Religion, like art, *lives* in so far as it is performed, i.e., in so far as its rituals are "going concerns." If you wish to spay or geld religion, first remove its rituals, its generative and regenerative processes. For religion is not a cognitive system, a set of dogmas, alone, it is meaningful experience and experienced meaning. In ritual one lives *through* events, or through the alchemy of its framings and symbolings, *re*lives semiogenetic events, the deeds and words of prophets and saints, or if these are absent, myths and sacred epics.

If, then, we regard narrative as an "emic" Western genre or meta-genre of expressive culture, it has to be seen as one of the cultural grandchildren or great-grandchildren of "tribal" ritual or juridical process. But if we regard narrative, "etically," as the supreme instrument for binding the "values" and "goals," in Dilthey's sense of these terms, which motivate human conduct, particularly when men and women become actors in social drama, into situational structures of "meaning," then we must concede it to be a universal cultural activity, embedded in the very center of the social drama, itself another cross-cultural and trans-temporal unit of social process. "Narrate" is from the Latin *narrare*, "to tell," which is akin to the

Latin *gnarus*, "knowing, acquainted with, expert in," both derivative from the Indo-European root, *GNA*, to "know," whence the vast family of words deriving from the Latin *cognoscere*, including "cognition" itself, and "noun" and "pronoun," the Greek *gignōskein*, whence *gnosis*, and the Old English past participle *gecnawan*, whence the Modern English, "know." Narrative is, it would seem, rather an appropriate term for a reflexive activity which seeks to "know" (even in its ritual aspect, to have *gnōsis* about) antecedent events, and about the meaning of those events. *Drama* itself is, of course, derived from the Greek *dran*, "to do, or act," hence narrative is knowledge (and/or *gnosis*) emerging from action, i.e., experiential knowledge. The redressive phase of social drama frames an endeavor to re-articulate a social group broken by sectional or self-serving interests; in like manner, the narrative component in ritual and legal action attempts to re-articulate opposing values and goals in a meaningful structure, the plot of which makes cultural sense. Where historical life itself fails to make cultural sense in terms that formerly held good, narrative and cultural drama may have the task of *poiesis*, that is, of remaking cultural sense, even when they seem to be dismantling ancient edifices of meaning, that can no longer redress our modern "dramas of living"—now ever more on a global and species-threatening scale.

References

Belmont, Nicole. *Arnold Van Gennep: The Creator of French Ethnography*. Trans. by Derek Coltman. Chicago: Chicago University Press, 1979.

Bercovitch, Sacvan. *The American Jeremiad*. Madison: University of Wisconsin Press, 1978.

Gennep, Arnold van. *The Rites of Passage*. London: Routledge and Kegan Paul, 1960. First published 1908.

Grathoff, R. *The Structure of Social Inconsistencies: A Contribution to a Unifed Theory of Play, Game and Social Action*. The Hague: Martinus Nijhoff, 1970.

Handelman, Don. "Is Naven Ludic?" *Social Analysis* (published in Adelaide, Australia), no. 1, 1979.

Hanna, Judith Lynne. *To Dance is Human: A Theory of Nonverbal Communication*. Austin: University of Texas Press, 1979.

Heusch, Luc de. *Le roi ivre ou l'origine de l'Etat*. Paris: Gallimard, 1972.

Hodges, H.A. *The Philosophy of Wilhelm Dilthey*. London: Routledge and Kegan Paul, 1952.

Legesse, Asmarom. *Gada: Three Approaches to the Study of African Society.* New York: Free Press, 1973.

Moore, Sally Falk. *Law as Process.* London: Routledge and Kegan Paul, 1978.

Myerhoff, Barbara. *Life History among the Elderly: Performance, Visibility, and Remembering.* n.d.

—, and Moore, Sally Falk (eds.) *Secular Ritual.* Amsterdam: Royal van Gorcum, 1977.

Pike, Kenneth L. *Language in Relation to a Unified Theory of the Structure of Human Behavior.* Glendale, California: Summer Institute of Linguistics, 1954.

Rappaport, Roy. *Ecology, Meaning, and Religion.* Richmond, California: North American Books, 1979.

Sapir, Edward. "Emergence of a Concept of Personality in a Study of Cultures." *Journal of Social Psychology,* 5, pp. 410-416, 1934.

Spindler, George D. (ed.) *The Making of Psychological Anthropology.* Berkeley: University of California Press, 1978.

Turner, Victor. *Schism and Continuity in an African Society: A Study of Ndembu Village Life.* Manchester: Manchester University Press, 1957.

—. *The Forest of Symbols: Aspects of Ndembu Ritual.* Ithaca: Cornell University Press, 1967.

—. *The Drums of Afflictin: A Study of Religious Processes among the Ndembu of Zambia.* Oxford: The Clarendon Press, 1968.

—. *The Ritual Process: Structure and Anti-Structure.* Chicago: Aldine, 1969.

—. *Dramas, Fields, and Metaphors: Symbolic Action in Human Society.* Ithaca: Cornell University Press, 1974.

Vansina, Jan. *Kingdoms of the Savanna.* Madison: University of Wisconsin Press, 1966.

White, Hayden. *Metahistory: The Historical Imagination in Nineteenth-Century Europe.* Baltimore: Johns Hopkins University Press, 1973.

Dramatic Ritual/Ritual Drama

Performative and Reflexive
Anthropology

I've long thought that teaching and learning anthropology should be more fun than they often are. Perhaps we should not merely read and comment on ethnographies, but actually perform them. Alienated students spend many tedious hours in library carrels struggling with accounts of alien lives and even more alien anthropological theories about the ordering of those lives. Whereas anthropology should be about, in D.H. Lawrence's phrase, "man alive" and "woman alive," this living quality frequently fails to emerge from our pedagogics, perhaps, to cite Lawrence again, because our "analysis presupposes a corpse."

It is becoming increasingly recognized that the anthropological monograph is itself a rather rigid literary genre which grew out of the notion that in the human sciences reports must be modeled rather abjectly on those of the natural sciences. But such a genre has no privileged position, especially now that we realize that in social life cognitive, affective, and volitional elements are bound up with one another and are alike primary, seldom found in their pure form, often hybridized, and only comprehensible by the investigator as lived experience, *his/hers* as well as, and in relation to, *theirs*.

Even the best of ethnographic films fail to communicate much of what it means to *be* a member of the society filmed. A selected, often slanted, series of visual images is directed at a passive audience. Discussion in the classroom then centers on the items picked out for attention by the film maker. Though a good teacher will plausibly relate the movie to ethnographic contexts drawn from the literature, much of the sociocultural and psychological complexity of those contexts cannot be related to the film. Anthropological monographs and movies may describe or present the incentives to action characteristic of a given group, but only rarely will these genres catch up their readers or spectators fully into the culture's motivational web.

How, then, may this be done? One possibility may be to turn the more interesting portions of ethnographies into playscripts, then to act them out in class, and finally to turn back to ethnographies armed with the understanding that comes from "getting inside the skin" of members of other cultures, rather than merely "taking the role of the other" in one's own culture. A whole new set of problems is generated by this apparently simple process. For each of its three stages (ethnography into playscript, script into performance, performance into meta-ethnography) reveals many of the frailties of anthropology, that essentially Western traditional discipline. And the process forces us to look beyond purely anthropological accounts—to literature, history, biography, incidents of travel—for data that may contribute to convincing playscripts. Where social dramas do find their cultural "doubles" (to reverse Antonin Artaud) in aesthetic dramas and other genres of cultural performance, there may well develop, as Richard Schechner has argued, a convergence betwen them, so that the processual form of social dramas is implicit in aesthetic dramas (even if only by reversal or negation), while the *rhetoric* of social dramas—and hence the shape of argument—is drawn from cultural performances. There was a lot of Perry Mason in Watergate!

The "playing" of ethnography is a genuinely interdisciplinary enterprise, for if we are to satisfy ourselves of the reliability of our script and our performance of it, we will need advice from various nonanthropological sources. Professionals in the field of drama in our own culture—scriptwriters, directors, actors, even stagehands—draw on centuries of professional experience in performing plays. Ideally, we need to consult, better still, bring in as part of the cast, members of the culture being enacted. We may, sometimes, be lucky enough to enlist the aid of theatrical or folk professionals from the society we are studying. But, in any case, those who know the business from the inside can help enormously.

I was given an opportunity to test these speculations in practice when, with fellow social scientists Alexander Alland and Erving Goffman, I was invited by Richard Schechner to take part in what was called "an intensive workshop" to "explore the interface between ritual and the theatre . . . between social and aesthetic drama," and other limina between the social sciences and performing arts. I had often thought about the relationship between processual forms of social conflict in many societies, described by anthropologists and genres of cultural performance. Several years earlier, mutual friends had made me aware of Schechner's interest in the same problem from the viewpoint of theatre. The collaboration of Colin Turnbull (*The Mountain People*, 1972) and Peter Brook which converted Turnbull's study of the Ik of Uganda into a series of dramatic episodes alerted me to the possibility of turning suitable ethnographic data into playscripts. That experiment persuaded me that cooperation between anthropological and theatrical people was not only possible but also could become a major teaching tool for both sets of partners in a world many of whose components are beginning to want to know one another. If it is true that we learn something about ourselves from taking the role of others, anthropologists, those cultural brokers *par excellence,* might be challenged to make this an intercultural as well as an intracultural enterprise.

Though many social scientists frown on the terms *performance* and *drama*, they seem to be central. *Performance*, as we have seen, is derived from the Middle English *parfournen*, later *parfourmen*, which is itself from the Old French *parfournir—par* ("thoroughly") plus *fournir* ("to furnish")—hence *performance* does not necessarily have the structuralist implication of manifesting *form*, but rather the processual sense of "bringing to completion" or "accomplishing." To *perform* is thus to complete a more or less involved process rather than to do a single deed or act. To *perform* ethnography, then, is to bring the data home to us in their fullness, in the plenitude of their action-meaning. Cognitive reductionism has always struck me as a kind of dehydration of social life. Sure, the patterns can be elicited, but the wishes and emotions, the personal and collective goals and strategies, even the situational vulnerabilities, weariness, and mistakes are lost in the attempt to objectify and produce an aseptic theory of human behavior modeled essentially on eighteenth century "scientific" axioms of belief about mechanical causality. Feelings and desires are not a pollution of cognitive pure essence, but close to what we humanly are; if anthropology is to become a true science of human action, it must take them just as seriously as the structures which sometimes perhaps represent the exhausted husks of action bled of its motivations.

The term *drama* has been criticized (by Max Gluckman and Raymond Firth, for example) as the imposition on observational data of a schema derived from *cultural* genres, hence "loaded" and not "neutral" enough for scientific use (Gluckman, 1977:227-43; Firth, 1974:1-2). I have to disagree, for my notebooks are filled with descriptions of day-to-day events which, added together, undeniably possess dramatic form, representing a course of action. Let me try to describe what I mean by *drama*, specifically *social drama*. (For a fuller account of my theory of the social drama see my

Schism and Continuity in an African Society, 1957, and Chapter Three above.)

I hold that the social drama form occurs on all levels of social organization from state to family. A social drama is initiated when the peaceful tenor of regular, norm-governed social life is interrupted by the *breach* of a rule controlling one of its salient relationships. This leads swiftly or slowly to a state of *crisis*, which, if not soon sealed off, may split the community into contending factions and coalitions. To prevent this, *redressive* means are taken by those who consider themselves or are considered the most legitimate or authoritative representatives of the relevant community. Redress usually involves ritualized action, whether legal (in formal or informal courts), religious (involving beliefs in the retributive action of powerful supernatural entities, and often involving an act of sacrifice), or military (for example, feuding, headhunting, or engaging in organized warfare). If the situation does not regress to *crisis* (which may remain endemic until some radical restructuring of social relationships, sometimes by revolutionary means, is undertaken), the next phase of social drama comes into play, which involves alternative solutions to the problem. The first is *reconciliation* of the conflicting parties following judicial, ritual, or military processes; the second, *consensual recognition of irremediable breach,* usually followed by the spatial separation of the parties. Since social dramas suspend normal everyday role playing, they interrupt the flow of social life and force a group to take cognizance of its own behavior in relation to its own values, even to question at times the value of those values. In other words, dramas induce and contain reflexive processes and generate cultural frames in which reflexivity can find a legitimate place.

With this processual form as a rough guide for our work at Schechner's summer institute, I tried to involve anthropology and drama students in the joint task of writing scripts for and performing ethnographies. It seemed best to choose parts of classical ethnographies that lent themselves to dramatic treatment, such as Malinowski's *Crime and Custom*, with its young man threatening suicide from a treetop when his father's matrilineal kin urged him to leave their village on his father's death (*Crime and Custom*, 1926: p. 78). But time being short (we had only two weeks), I had to fall back upon my own ethnography both because I knew it best, and because I had already, to some extent, written a script for a substantial amount of field data in the form I have called *social drama*. My wife, Edie, and I tried to explain to a group of about a dozen students and teachers, almost equally divided between anthropology and drama, what cultural assumptions lay behind the first two social dramas that I described in my book *Schism and Continuity in An African Society* (pp. 95, 116). It was not enough to give them a few cognitive models or structural principles. We had to try to create the illusion of what it is to live Ndembu village life. Could this possibly be done with a few bold strokes, with a gesture or two? Of course not, but there may be ways of getting people bodily as well as mentally involved in another (not physically present) culture.

The setting for all this was an upper room in the Performing Garage, a theatre in Soho where Schechner's company, The Performance Group, has given some notable performances, including *Dionysus in 69, Makbeth, Mother Courage,* and, more recently, the *Tooth of Crime* and *Rumstick Road* (directed by Elizabeth LeCompte). I knew that Schechner set great store on what he calls the "rehearsal process," which essentially consists of establishing a dynamic relationship, over whatever time it takes, among playscript, actors, director, stage, and props, with no initial presumptions about the primacy of any of these. Sessions often have no time limit; in some, exercises of various kinds, including breathing exercises to loosen up actors, may go on for an hour or so; in others, players may cast themselves rather than be cast by the director. In this complex process, Schechner sees the actor, in taking the role of another—provided by a playscript—as moving, under the intuitive and experienced eye of the director/producer, from the "not-me" (the blueprinted role) to the "not-not-me" (the realized role), and he sees the movement itself as constituting a kind of liminal phase in which all kinds of experiential experiments are possible, indeed mandatory. This is a different style of acting from that which relies on superb professional technique to imitate almost any Western role with verisimilitude. Schechner aims at *poiesis,* rather than *mimesis:* making, not faking. The role grows along with the actor, it is truly "created" through the rehearsal process which may sometimes involve painful moments of self-revelation. Such a method is particularly appropriate for anthropological teaching because the "mimetic" method will work only on familiar material (Western models of behavior), whereas the "poietic," since it recreates behavior from within, can handle unfamiliar material.

In an experimental session convoked by Schechner to rehearse Ibsen's *Doll House,* for example, we came up with four Noras, one of whom actually made a choice contrary to Ibsen's script. It happened that in her personal life she herself was being confronted with a dilemma similar to Nora's: should she separate from her husband, leave her two children with him (he wanted this), and embark upon an independent career? In reliving her own problem through enacting Nora's, she began to wring her hands in a peculiarly poignant, slow, complex way. Eventually, instead of detonating the famous door slam that some critics say ushered in modern theatre, she rushed back to the group, signifying that she was not ready—at least not yet—to give up her children, thus throwing unexpected light on the ethical toughness of Ibsen's Nora. Schechner said that the hand-wringing was "the bit of reality" he would preserve from that particular rehearsal and embody in the Nora-role in subsequent rehearsals. As these succeeded one another, a bricolage of such gestures, incidents, renderings of not-self into not-not-self would be put together and molded artistically into a processual unity. Depth, reflexivity, a haunting ambiguity may thus be infused into a series of performances, each a unique event.

Particularly since I had no skill or experience in direction, the task of communicating to the actors the setting and atmosphere of daily life in a very different culture proved quite formidable. In one's own society an actor tries to realize "individual character," but takes partly for granted the culturally defined roles supposedly played by that character: father, businessman, friend, lover, fiancé, trade union leader, farmer, poet, and so on. These roles are made up of collective representations shared by actors and audience, who are usually members of the same culture. By contrast, an actor who enacts ethnography has to learn the cultural rules behind the roles played by the character he is representing. How is this to be done? Not, I think, by reading monographs in abstraction from performance, *then* performing the part. There must be a dialectic between performing and learning. One learns through performing, then performs the understandings so gained.

I decided *faute de mieux* to give a reading performance myself of the first two social dramas, interpolating explanatory comments whenever it seemed necessary. The group had already read the relevant pages from *Schism and Continuity*. The dramas were broadly about Ndembu village politics, competition for headmanship, ambition, jealousy, sorcery, the recruiting of factions, and the stigmatizing of rivals, particularly as these operated within a local group of matrilineally related kin and some of their relations by marriage and neighbors. I had collected a number of accounts of these dramas from participants in them. My family and I had lived in the village that was their "stage" or "arena" for at least fifteen months and knew it well during the whole period of my field work—almost two-and-a-half years.

When I had finished reading the drama accounts, the actors in the workshop told me at once that they needed to be "put in the right mood"; to "sense the atmospherics" of Ndembu village life. One of them had brought some records of Yoruba music, and, though this is a different musical idiom from Central African music, I led them into a dancing circle, showing them to the best of my limited, arthritic ability, some of the moves of Ndembu dancing. This was fun, but off-center fun. It then occurred to us that we might recreate with the limited props available to us in the theatre the key redressive ritual which was performed in the second social drama, and whose form we knew very well from having taken part in it on several occasions. This ritual, "name inheritance" (*Kuswanika ijina*), was an emotional event, for it marked the temporary end of a power struggle between the stigmatized candidate for headmanship, Sandombu, and Mukanza, the successful candidate, and his immediate matrilineal kin. Sandombu had been driven by public pressure from the village for a year, for it was alleged that he had killed by sorcery Nyamuwaha, a cousin on his mother's side whom he called "mother," a much loved old lady, sister of Mukanza. Sandombu had shed tears on being accused (even his former foes admitted this), but he had been in exile for a year. As time went by, members of the village remembered how, as a foreman, he had helped them find paid labor in the public works department road gang, and how he had always been generous with food and beer to guests. The pretext to invite him back came when a minor epidemic of illness broke out in the village while at the same time many people dreamed frequently of Nyamuwaha. Divination found that her shade was disturbed by the troubles in the village. To appease her, a quickset sapling of *muyombu* tree, a species for memorializing the lineage dead, was to be planted for her. Sandombu was invited to do the ritual planting. He also paid the village a goat in compensation for his angry behavior the previous year. The ritual marked his reincorporation into the village, even though formally it had to do with the inheritance of Nyamuwaha's name by her oldest daughter, Manyosa (who afterwards became my wife's best friend in the village).

Stirred by the dancing and recorded drumming, I was moved to try to recreate the name-inheritance rite in Soho. For the *muyombu* tree, I found as substitute a brush handle. For ritual "white" beer as libation, a cup of water would have to do. There was no white clay to anoint people with, but I found some clear white salt, which I moistened. And to pare the top of the brush handle, as Ndembu shrine trees are pared to reveal the white wood under the bark (an operation symbolically related to the purification that is circumcision), I found a sharp kitchen knife. Afterwards, I was told by one of the group that she was terrified that I would do something "grisly" with it! But truly there is often some element of risk or danger in the atmosphere of living ritual. And something numinous.

To translate this very specific Ndembu rite into modern American terms, I took the role of the new village headman, and with my wife's help prepared the surrogate *muyombu* shrine-tree with knife and salt, and "planted" it in a crack in the floor. The next move was to persuade someone to play Manyosa's role in this situation. Someone whom we shall call Becky, a professional director of drama, volunteered.

I asked Becky to give me the name of a recently deceased close female relative of an older generation who had meant much in her life. Considerably moved, she mentioned her mother's sister Ruth. I then prayed in Chilunda to "village ancestors." Becky sat beside me before the "shrine," her legs extended in front of her, her head bowed in the Ndembu position of ritual modesty. I then anointed the shrine-tree with the improvised *mpemba*, white clay, symbol of unity with the ancestors and the living community, and drew three lines with it on the ground, from the shrine to myself. I then anointed Becky by the orbits of her eyes, on the brow, and above the navel. I declared her to be "Nswana-Ruth," "successor of Ruth," in a way identified with Ruth, in another replacing her, though not totally, as a structural persona. I repeated the anointing process with other members of the group, not naming them after deceased kin but joining them into the symbolic unity of our recently formed community of teachers and students. Then, Edie and I tied strips of white cloth around everyone's brows, and I poured out another libation of the white beer at the base of the shrine-tree. There was clearly a double symbolism here, for I was using Western substances to represent Ndembu objects which themselves had symbolic value in ritual, making of them, as it were, situational indices of cultural symbols. Surely, at so many removes, must not the whole performance have seemed highly artificial, inauthentic? Oddly enough, according to the students, it did not.

The workshop group later reported that they had gone on discussing what had occurred for several hours. They agreed that the enactment of the Ndembu ritual was the turning point which brought to them both the affectual structure of the social drama and the tension between factionalism and scapegoatism, on the one hand, and the deep sense of village "belonging together" on the other. It also showed them how an enhanced collective and individual understanding of the conflict situation could be achieved by participating in a ritual performance with its kinesiological as well as cognitive codes.

In the following days, the group began work on the actual staging of the ritual dramas. One suggestion favored a dualistic approach: some events (for example, when Sandombu, the ambitious claimant, having killed an antelope, gave only a small portion of meat to his mother's brother, the headman) would be treated realistically, naturalistically; but the world of cultural beliefs, particularly those connected with sorcery and the ancestor cult, would be treated symbolically. For example, it was widely believed, not only by Sandombu's village opponents but also in Ndembu society at large, that Sandombu had killed the headman by paying a powerful sorcerer to summon up from a stream a familiar spirit in the shape of a human-faced serpent, owned by (and also owning) the headman, and by shooting it with his "night-gun," a musket carved from a human tibia and primed with graveyard earth. Such snake-familiars, or *malomba*, are thought to have the faces of their owners and to creep about the village at night invisibly, listening, in wiretap fashion, to derogatory remarks made about their owners by rivals. They grow by eating their shadows, or life-principles, of their owners' foes, who are usually their owners' kin. They function as a kind of Frazerian "external soul," but when they are destroyed by magical means, such as the night-gun, their owners are destroyed too. Chiefs and headmen have "strong *malomba*," and it takes strong medicine to kill them.

Our class suggested that Sandombu's *ilomba* familiar (that is, his quasi-paranoid underself) should be presented as a kind of chorus to the play. Being privy to the political plotting in the situation, the *ilomba* could tell the audience (in the manner of Shakespeare's Richard the Third) what was going on under the surface of kinship-norm-governed relationships in the village. One suggestion was that we make a film, to be shown in the background, of an *ilomba* cynically disclosing the "real" structure of political power relationships, as known to him, while the dramatis personae of the social drama, on stage and in the foreground, behaved with formal restraint towards one another, with an occasional outburst of authentic hostile feeling.

During the discussion, a graduate student in anthropology gave the drama students in the group some cogent instruction in the nature of matrilineal kinship systems and problems, and, later, in the Ndembu system which combined matrilineal descent with virilocal marriage (residence at the husband's village), and asserted the dominance of succession of brothers to office over the succession of the sister's son—one of the causes of dispute in Mukanza village where the dramas were set. This invocation of cognitive models proved helpful, but only because the nonanthropologists had been stimulated to *want* to know them by the enactment of some Ndembu ritual and the witnessing of the dramatic narrative of political struggle in a matrilineal social context.

To give a more personal idea of the values associated by the Ndembu with matrilineal descent, my wife read to the women of the whole class a piece she had written about the girls' puberty ritual of the Ndembu. I had described this ritual somewhat dryly in the conventional anthropological mode in my book *The Drums of Affliction* (1968: chaps. VII-VIII). Her account, however, grew from participation in an intersubjective world of women involved in this complex ritual sequence, and communicated vividly the feelings and wishes of women in this *rite de passage* in a matrilineal society. Trying to capture the affective dimension the reading revealed, the women in the drama section of the workshop attempted a new technique of staging. They began a rehearsal with a ballet, in which women created a kind of frame with their bodies, positioning themselves to form a circle, in which the subsequent male political action could take place. Their idea was to show that action went on within a matrilineal sociocultural space.

Somehow this device didn't work—there was a covert contemporary political tinge in it which denatured the Ndembu sociocultural process. This feminist mode of staging ethnography assumed and enacted modern ideological notions in a situation in which those ideas are simply irrelevant. The Ndembu struggles were dominated by individual clashes of will and personal and collective emotional responses concerned with assumed or alleged breaches of entitlement. What was dominant was not the general matrilineal structures of inheritance, succession, and social placement in lineages but rather will, ambition, and political goals. The matrilineal structures influenced the tactics used by contestants overmastered by their will to obtain temporal power, but politics was mainly in the hands of males. A script should thus focus on power-struggling rather than matrilineal assumptions if it is to stay true to the ethnography. But perhaps the ethnography itself should be put in question? This was one view some of our female class members raised. And, indeed, such a question is legitimate when one opens ethnographies out to the performative process. Does a male ethnographer, like myself, really understand or take into full analytical account the nature of matrilineal structure and its embodiment, not only in women but also in men, as a powerful factor in all their actions—political, legal, kinship, ritual, economic?

Nevertheless, the fact remained that political office, even in this matrilineal society, was largely a male affair, if not a male monopoly. Hence, the attempt to bring into the foreground the female framing of Ndembu society diverted attention from the fact that these particular dramas were essentially male political struggles—even though conducted in terms of matrilineal descent. The real tragedy of Sandombu was not that he was embedded in a matrilineal structure (whether matrilineal, patrilineal, or bilateral) which played down individual political gifts and played up advantages derived from positions assigned by birth. In capitalistic America, or socialistic Russia or China, a political animal like Sandombu might have thrived. In Ndembu vilage politics, however, a person with ambition, but procreatively sterile and without many matrilineal kin, was almost from the start a doomed man.

The trouble was that time ran out before the group had a chance to portray Sandombu's situation. But all of us, in anthropology and drama, now had a problem to think about. How could we turn ethnography into script, *then* enact that script, *then* think about,*then* go back to fuller ethnography, *then* make a new script, *then* act it again? This interpretive circulation between data, praxis, theory, and more data—a kind of hermeneutical Catherine wheel, if you like—provides a merciless critique of ethnography. There is nothing like acting the part of a member of another culture in a crisis situation characteristic of that culture to detect inauthenticity in the reporting usually made by Westerners and to raise problems undiscussed or unresolved in the ethnographic narrative. However, this very deficiency may have pedagogical merit insofar as it motivates the student/actor to read more widely in the literature on the culture.

It is hard, furthermore, to separate aesthetic and performative problems from anthropological interpretations. The most incisively or plainly reported extended case histories contained in ethnographies still have to be further distilled and abbreviated for the purposes of performance. To do this tellingly and effectively, sound knowledge of the salient sociocultural contexts must combine with presentational skills to produce an effective playscript, one which effectively portrays both individual psychology and social process articulated in terms of the models provided by a particular culture. One advantage of scripting ethnography in this way is that it draws attention to cultural subsystems, such as that constituted by witchcraft/divination/performance of redressive ritual, in a dramatic way. The workshop group's suggestion that a film or ballet should be performed in the background of the naturalistic drama portraying the *ilomba* and other creatures of witchcraft (masks and masquerading could be employed) might be an effective device for revealing the hidden, perhaps even unconscious levels of action. It would also act as a vivid set of footnotes on the cultural assumptions of the Ndembu dramatis personae.

Our experience of the theatre workshop suggested a number of guidelines for how collaboration between anthropologists and practitioners of drama and dance, at whatever stage of training, might be undertaken. First of all, anthropologists might present to their drama colleagues a series of ethnographic texts selected for their performative potential. The processed ethnotext would then be transformed into a workable preliminary playscript. Here the know-how of theatre people—their sense of dialogue; understanding of setting and props; ear for a telling, revelatory phrase—could combine with the anthropologist's understanding of cultural meanings, indigenous rhetoric, and material culture. The playscript, of course, would be subject to continuous modification during the rehearsal process, which would lead up to an actual performance. At this stage, we would need an experienced director, preferably one familiar with anthropology and with non-Western theatre (like Schechner or Peter Brook), and certainly familiar with the social structure and the rules and themes underlying the surface structures of the culture being enacted. There would be a constant back-and-forth movement from anthropological analysis of the ethnography, which provides the details for enactment, to the synthesizing and integrating activity of dramatic composition, which would include sequencing scenes, relating the words and actions of the characters to previous and future events, and rendering actions in appropriate stage settings. For in this kind of ethnographic drama, it is not only the individual characters who have dramatic importance but also the deep processes of social life. From the anthropological viewpoint, there is drama indeed in the working out and mutual confrontation of sociocultural processes. Sometimes, even, the actors on the stage almost seem puppets on processual strings.

Students of anthropology could also help drama students during rehearsal itself, if not by direct participation, at least in the role of *Dramaturg*, a position founded by Lessing in eighteenth-century Germany and defined by Richard Hornby as "simply a literary advisor to the [theater] director" (*Script into Performance*, 1977:63). Hornby and Schechner envision the *Dramaturg* as a sort of structuralist literary critic who carries on his research through a production rather than merely in his study (pp. 197-199). But the anthropological *Dramaturg* or *Ethnodramaturg* is not so much concerned with the *structure* of the playscript (itself a definite move from ethnography to literature) as with the fidelity of that script to both the described facts and the anthropological analysis of the structures and processes of the group. Incidentally, I am not calling for a mandatory exclusion of anthropologists from the acting role! Indeed, I think that participation in this role would significantly enhance anthropologists' "scientific" understanding of the culture being studied in this dynamic fashion, for human science is concerned, as we have said, with "man alive." But I am aware of the evasiveness and voyeurism of my kind—which we rationalize as "objectivity." Perhaps we need a little more of the dsciplined abandonment that theatre demands! However, as second best, we can settle for the role of *Ethnodramaturg*.

The movement from ethnography to performance is a process of pragmatic reflexivity. Not the reflexivity of a narcissistic isolate moving among his or her memories and dreams, but the attempt of representatives of one generic modality of human existence, the Western historical experience, to understand "on the pulses," in Keatsian metaphor, other modes hitherto locked away from it by cognitive chauvinism or cultural snobbery.

Historically, ethnodramatics is emerging just when knowledge is being increased about other cultures, other world views, other life styles; when Westerners, endeavoring to trap non-Western philosophies, dramatics, and poetics in the corrals of their own cognitive constructions, find that they have caught sublime monsters, Eastern dragons who are lords of fructile chaos, whose wisdom makes our cognitive knowledge look somehow shrunken, shabby, and inadequate to our new apprehension of the human condition.

Cartesian dualism has insisted on separating subject from object, us from them. It has, indeed, made voyeurs of Western man, exaggerating sight by macro- and micro-instrumentation, the better to learn the structures of the world with an "eye" to its exploitation. The deep bonds between body and mentality, unconscious and conscious thinking, species and self have been treated without respect, as though irrelevant for analytical purposes.

The reflexivity of performance dissolves these bonds and so creatively democratizes: as we become on earth a single noosphere, the Platonic cleavage between an aristocracy of the spirit and the "lower or foreign orders" can no longer be maintained. To be reflexive is to be at once one's own subject and direct object. The poet, whom Plato rejected from his *Republic*, subjectivizes the object, or, better, makes intersubjectivity the characteristically postmodern human mode.

It is perhaps perfectly natural that an anthropology of performance should be moving to meet dramatic performers who are seeking some of their theoretical support from anthropology. With the renewed emphasis on society as a process punctuated by performances of various kinds, there has developed the view that such genres as ritual, ceremony, carnival, festival, game, spectacle, parade, and sports event may constitute, on various levels and in various verbal and nonverbal codes, a set of intersecting metalanguages. The group or community does not merely "flow" in unison at these performances, but, more actively, tries to understand itself in order to change itself. This dialectic between "flow" and reflexivity characterizes performative genres: a successful performance in any of the genres transcends the opposition between spontaneous and self-conscious patterns of action.

If anthropologists are ever to take ethnodramatics seriously, our discipline will have to become something more than a cognitive game played in our heads and inscribed in—let's face it—somewhat tedious journals. We will have to become performers ourselves, and bring to human, existential fulfillment what have hitherto been only mentalistic protocols. We must find ways of overcoming the boundaries of both political and cognitive structures by dramatistic empathy, sympathy, friendship, even love as we acquire ever deeper structural knowledge in reciprocity with the increasingly self-aware *ethnoi, barbaroi, goyim,* heathens, and marginals in pursuit of common tasks and rare imaginative transcendences of those tasks.

References

Firth, Raymond. "Society and its Symbols," *Times Literary Supplement,* pp. 1-2, September 13, 1974.

Gluckman, Max. "On Drama, and Games and Athletic Contests." In *Secular Ritual.* ed. S. Moore and B. Myerhoff, Assen, Holland: Royal van Gorcum, pp. 227-243, 1977.

Hornby, Richard. *Script into Performance.* Austin and London: University of Texas Press, 1977.

Turner, Victor. *Schism and Continuity in an African Society.* Manchester: Manchester University Press, 1957.

Acting in Everyday Life
and
Everyday Life in Acting

Acting, like all "simple" Anglo-Saxon words, is ambiguous—it can mean doing things in everyday life, or performing on the stage or in a temple. It can take place in ordinary time or in extraordinary time. It may be a way of working or moving, like a body's or machine's "action"; or it may be the art or occupation of performing in plays. It may be the essence of sincerity—the commitment of the self to a line of action for ethical motives perhaps to achieve "personal truth," or it may be the essence of pretence—when one "plays a part" in order to conceal or dissimulate. The former is the ideal of Jerzy Grotowski's "Poor Theatre"; the latter happens every day "at work." A spy, con-man, an *agent provocateur*—each of these has skill in "acting." The same person, in different situations, in a single day, can "put on" an act, or "act divinely." Yet these opposites coincide in our common parlance; we speak of "playing a role," when we intend a reference to some civically *serious* activity, such as an advisory role to a president. On the other hand, we talk of "great acting" on the stage as the source of some of our deepest "truest" understandings of the human condition. Acting is therefore both work and play, solemn and ludic, pretence or earnest, our mundane trafficking and commerce and what we do or behold in ritual or theatre. The very word "ambiguity" is derived from the Latin *agere* to "act" for it comes from the verb *ambigere*, to "wander," *ambi-*, "about, around" + *agere*, "to do," resulting in the sense of having two or more possible meanings, "moving from side to side," "of doubtful nature." In both major senses, doing deeds and performing, it is indispensable to mental health; as William Blake said: "He who nourishes Desires but *Acts* not, breeds Pestilence," a doublet "Proverb of Hell" to, "Expect Poison from the standing Water." In Western languages, action has also the flavor of contestation. Action is "agonistic." *Act, agon, agony,* and *agitate* are all derived from the same Indo-European base **ag-,* "to drive," from which came the Latin *agere,* to do, and the Greek *agein* (ἄγει ✔), to lead. In Western (Euro-American) culture, work and play both have this driving, conflictive character, which long precedes Max Weber's famed Protestant ethic. In those genres of *cultural* performance which predated Greek theatre—for example, myth-recitation, ritual, oral epic or saga, and the telling and acting of lays and *märchen*—wars and feuds between groups of deities or clans and lineages headed by well-armed heroes, as well as competition for position, power, or scarce resources, men's conflict over women, and divisions between close kin were vividly portrayed, carried out in mimicry.

Phyllis Hartnoll (*The Concise History of Theater,* n.d.: p.8) writes of the development of Greek tragedy from the dithyramb (or unison hymn) sung around the altar of Dionysus during certain religious feasts. The dithyramb, originally in lyric form, a praise song for Dionysus, came to deal with his life and mythos in much the same way as early medieval European liturgical plays about the birth, life, and resurrection of Christ, narratives loaded with conflict, grew from the lyrical portion of the Easter morning mass. The Mass, the Eucharist, itself was, of course, a drama with a scriptural script long before it gave rise to "Passion Plays." The Greek dithyramb expanded to embrace not only Dionysian tales, but also those of gods, demigods, and heroes, some of whom were regarded as the founding ancestors of the Hellenes and their Mediterranean neighbors. "The deeds of these heroes, good or bad," writes Hartnoll (*ibid*: 8-9), "their wars, feuds, marriages and adulteries, and the destinies of their children, who so often suffered for the sins of their parents, are a source of dramatic tension, and gives rise to the essential element of conflict—between man and god, good and evil, child and parent, duty and inclination. This may lead to comprehension and reconciliation between the conflicting elements—since a Greek tragedy need not necessarily end unhappily—or to incomprehension and chaos. The plots of all Greek plays were already well known to the audience. They formed part of its religious and cultural heritage, for many of them dated from Homeric times. The interest for the spectator lay, therefore, not in the novelty of the story, but in seeing how the dramatist had chosen to deal with it, and no doubt, in assessing the quality of the acting, and the work of the chorus, both in singing and dancing, about which unfortunately we know very little."

Hartnoll's summary is correct—as far as it goes. But it does not mention the important fact that the plays—Aristophanes' comedies as much as

Aeschylus' and Sophocles' tragedies—in Geertz's terms are "social metacommentaries" on contemporaneous Greek society, that is, whatever the nature of their plot, whether drawn from myths or reputed historical accounts, they were intensely "reflexive." If they were "mirrors held up to nature" (or rather to society and culture) they were *active* (that propulsive word again!) mirrors, mirrors that probed and analyzed the axioms and assumptions of the social structure, isolated the building blocks of the culture, and sometimes used them to construct novel edifices, Cloud Cuckoolands or Persian courts that never were on land or sea, but were, nevertheless, possible variants based on rules underlying the structures of familiar sociocultural life or experienced social reality.

Theatre is perhaps the most forceful, *active*, if you like, genre of cultural performance, but there are many others, some of which I have mentioned. No society is without some mode of metacommentary—Geertz's illuminating phrase for a "story a group tells itself about itself" or in the case of theatre, a play a society acts about itself—not only a reading of its experience but an interpretive reenactment of its experience. In the simpler, preindustrial societies, there are often complex systems of ritual—initiatory, seasonal, curative, and divinatory—which act, so to speak, not only as means of "reanimating sentiments of social solidarity" as an older generation of anthropologists would put it, but also as scanning devices whereby the difficulties and conflicts of the present are articulated and given meaning through contextualization in an abiding cosmological scheme. The anger of gods or ancestors may be proposed as the cause of present misfortune, anger aroused by some blatant or persistent transgression of customs handed down from high antiquity and vouched for by revered origin myths. In complex, large-scale societies, in which the sphere of leisure is clearly separated from that of work, innumerable genres of cultural performance arise in accordance with the principle of the division of labor. These may be labeled art, entertainment, sport, play, games, recreation, theatre, light or serious reading, and many more. They may be collective or private, amateur or professional, slight or serious. Not all of them have the reflexive character of many Greek plays. Not all of them have universal reference, for many are limited to specific constituencies (men, women, children, rich, poor, intellectual, middlebrow, and so on). But in this prolixity of genres, now given wider scope by the electronic media, some seem more effective than others in giving birth to self-regulatory or self-critical works, which catch the attention, or fire the imagination, of an entire society or even of an epoch, transcending national frontiers. In a complex culture it might be possible to regard the ensemble of performative and narrative genres, active and acting modalities of expressive culture as a hall of mirrors, or better magic mirrors (plane, convex, concave, convex cylinder, saddle or matrix mirrors to borrow metaphors from the study of reflecting surfaces) in which social problems, issues, and crises (from *causes célèbres* to changing macrosocial categorial relations between the sexes and age groups) are reflected as diverse images, transformed, evaluated, or diagnosed in works typical of each genre, then shifted to another genre better able to scrutinize certain of their aspects, until many facets of the problem have been illuminated and made accessible to conscious remedial action. In this hall of mirrors the reflections are multiple, some magnifying, some diminishing, some distorting the faces peering into them, but in such a way as to provoke not merely thought, but also powerful feelings and the will to modify everyday matters in the minds of the gazers. For no one likes to see himself as ugly, ungainly, or dwarfish. Mirror distortions of reflection provoke reflexivity. In a fascinating article entitled "Mirror Images," (*Scientific American*, 1980:206-228) David Emil Thomas discusses how the mirror image is not always a faithful reflection; it can be inverted, reversed in handedness, or distorted in other ways. Thomas analyzes the transformations through a few basic curved mirrors, from which compound matrix mirrors are constructed: "by introducing various curvatures into reflecting surfaces, it is possible to create mirrors that change the shape, size, orientation, and handedness of the objects they reflect in dramatic and disturbing ways" (p. 206).

Theatre is perhaps closer to life than most performative genres, in that, despite its conventions and spatial restraints on physical possiblity, it is as Marjorie Boulton wrote, (*The Anatomy of Drama*, 1971:3) "literature that *walks* and *talks* before our eyes, meant to be performed, 'acted' we might say, rather than seen as marks on paper and sights, sounds, and action in our heads." Richard Schechner, in "Performers and Spectators Transported and Transformed" published in the *Kenyon Review*(1981:84) reminds us, however, that "performance behavior isn't free and easy. Performance behavior is known and/or practiced behavior or 'twice-behaved behavior,' 'restored behavior'— either rehearsed, previously known, learned by osmosis since early childhood, revealed during the performance by masters, guides, gurus, elders, or generated by rules that govern the outcomes as in improvisatory theatre or sports." Performance, then, is always doubled, the doubleness of acting as earlier discussed—it cannot escape reflection and reflexivity. This proximity of theatre to life, while remaining at a mirror distance from it, makes of it the form best fitted to comment or "meta-comment" on conflict, for life is conflict, of which contest is only a species. "Without Contraries is no Progression," as Blake said, if only in the sense that Life and Death, Eros and Thanatos, Yin and Yang, are in Freud's terms, "immortal antagonists"—incidentally another term in the *agere, agein, agōn* family. Even when, in certain kinds of theatre, in different cultures, conflict may appear to be muted or deflected or rendered as a playful or joyous struggle, it is not hard to detect threads of connection between elements of the play and sources of conflict in sociocultural milieus. The very mufflings and evasions of scenes of discord in some theatrical and natural traditions speak eloquently to their real presence in society, and may perhaps be regarded as a cultural defense-mechanism against conflict rather than a metacommentary upon it.

I might be supposed to have an intellectual vested interest in conflict and in drama as conflict, since I have discussed social conflict as "social drama" in several publications since my first book, *Schism and Continuity*, written a quarter of a century ago. Indeed, I have had to defend myself against such trenchant critics as my former teachers Sir Raymond Firth and the late Max Gluckman, who have accused me of unwarrantably introducing a model drawn from literature (they did not say *Western* literature, but clearly they had the Aristotelian model of tragedy in mind) to throw light on spontaneous social processes, which are not authored or set in conventions, but arise from clashes of interest or incompatible social structural principles in the give and take of everyday life in a social group. Recently, I have taken heart from an article by Geertz, "Blurred Genres: The Refiguration of Social Thought," (*American Scholar*, Spring 1980), which not only suggests "that analogies drawn from the humanities are coming to play the kind of role in sociological understanding that analogies drawn from the crafts and technology have long played in physical understanding" (p. 196), but also gives qualified approval to the "*drama* analogy for social life" (p. 172). Geertz numbers me among "proponents of the ritual theory of drama"—as against "the *symbolic action* approach" which stresses "the affinities of theater and rhetoric—drama as persuasion, the platform as stage" (p. 172), associated with Kenneth Burke. His pithy formulation of my position saves me the task of repeating my own. He writes: "For Turner, social dramas occur 'on all levels of social organization from state to family.' They arise out of conflict situations—a village falls into factions, a husband beats a wife, a region rises against the state—and proceed to their denouéments through publicly performed conventionalized behavior. As the conflict swells to crisis and the excited fluidity of heightened emotion, where people feel at once more enclosed in a common mood and loosened from their social moorings, ritualized forms of authority—litigation, feud, sacrifice, prayer—are invoked to contain it and render it orderly. If they succeed, the breach is healed and the status quo, or something resembling it, is restored; if they do not, it is accepted as incapable of remedy and things fall apart into various sorts of unhappy endings: migrations, divorces, or murders in the cathedral. With differing degrees of strictness and detail, Turner and his followers have applied this schema to tribal passage rites, curing ceremonies, and judicial processes; to Mexican insurrections, Icelandic sagas, and Thomas Becket's difficulties with Henry II; to picaresque narrative, millenarian movements, Caribbean carnivals, and Indian peyote hunts; and to the political upheaval of the Sixties. A form for all seasons."

This Parthian shaft leaps from Geertz's insistence in several of his writings that the social drama approach focuses too narrowly on "the *general movement* of things" (my italics) and neglects the multifarious cultural contents, the symbol systems which embody the ethos and eidos, the sentiments and values of *specific* cultures. He suggests that the "text analogy" (p. 175) can remedy this, that is, textual analysis attends to "how the *inscription* of action is brought about, what its *vehicles* are and how they work, and on what the *fixation* of meaning from the flow of events—*history* from what happened, *thought* from thinking, *culture* from behavior—implies for sociological interpretation. To see social institutions, social customs, social changes as in some sense 'readable' is to alter our whole sense of what such interpretation is towards modes of thought rather more familiar to the translator, the exegete, or the iconographer than to the test giver, the factor analyst, or the pollster" (pp. 175-176).

My answer to Geertz is simply to reiterate certain features of the social drama approach. He mentions "ritualized forms of authority—litigation, feud, sacrifice, prayer" that are used "to contain [crisis] and render it orderly." Such forms may crystallize any culture's *uniqueness,* are forms for particular seasons. For my part I have, indeed, often treated the ritual and juridical symbol systems of the Ndembu of Western Zambia as *text* analogues. But I have tried to locate these texts in *context* of *performance,* rather than to construe them into abstract, dominantly cognitive systems. However, Geertz does in fact concede that many anthropologists today, including himself, use *both* textual and dramatistic approaches, according to problem and context. Some of these misunderstandings and apparent contradictions can be resolved if we examine the relationship between the two modes of acting—in "real life" and "on stage"—as components of a dynamic system of interdependence between social dramas and cultural performances. Both dramatistic and textual analogies then fall into place.

Richard Schechner represented this relationship as a bisected figure eight laid on its side (see illus. p. 73 above). The two semicircles above the horizontal dividing line represent the manifest, visible public realm, those below it, the latent, hidden, perhaps even unconscious realm. The left loop or circlet represents social drama, divided into its four main phases, breach, crisis, redress, positive or negative denouement. The right loop represents a genre of cultural performance—for our purposes today, a stage of aesthetic drama. Notice that the manifest social drama feeds into the *latent* realm of stage drama; its characteristic form in a given culture, at a given time and place, unconsciously, or perhaps preconsciously, influences not only the form but also the content of the stage drama of which it is the active or "magic" mirror. The stage drama, when it is meant to do more than entertain—though entertainment is always one of its vital aims—is a metacommentary, explicit or implicit, witting or unwitting, on the major social dramas of its social context (wars, revolutions, scandals, institutional changes). Not only that, but its message and its rhetoric feed back into the

latent processual structure of the social drama and partly account for its
ready ritualization. Life itself now becomes a mirror held up to art, and the
living now *perform* their lives, for the protagonists of a social drama, a
"drama of living," have been equipped by aesthetic drama with some of
their most salient opinions, imageries, tropes, and ideological perspectives.
Neither mutual mirroring, life by art, art by life, is exact, for each is not a
planar mirror but a matricial mirror; at each exchange something new is
added, something old is lost or discarded. Human beings learn through experience, though all too often they repress painful experience, and perhaps
the deepest experience is through drama; *not* through social drama, or stage
drama (or its equivalent) *alone,* but in the circulatory or oscillatory process
of their mutual and incessant modification.

   If one were to guess at origins, my conjecture would be that *all* the genres
of cultural performance, from tribal rituals to TV "specials," are potentially present in the *third phase* of the generic social drama (which is like the
general mammalian condition that we still have with us throughout all the
global radiation of specific mammalian forms to fill special niches), the
phase of *redressive processes.* In a social drama, the first phase occurs when
one or more social norms regarded as binding and as sustaining key relationships between persons or sub-groups in a more or less bounded community are broken or all too obviously disregarded. Often there is a symbolic act drawing public attention to the *breach.* There is an act of civil
disobedience; a Boston Tea Party; an African hunter scorns and challenges
his village headman by refusing him the joint of meat that is his by
hereditary right; and the like. Once this occurs, no group member can turn
a blind eye to its implications. In the next phase, *crisis,* people take sides,
supporting either the rule-breaker or the target of his action. Factions,
coalitions, cabals are formed, heated language is exchanged, and actual
violence may occur. Former allies may be opposed, former foes united.
Conflict is usually contagious: old grudges are reanimated, old wounds
reopened, buried memories of victory or defeat in former struggles disinter-
red. For no social drama can ever be finally concluded: the terms of its ending are often the conditions under which a new one will arise. The unity
and continuity of the community may be menaced. All this may be "low
key" or "high key," the weapons may be stares, gestures, words, fisticuffs,
spears, or firearms. When the community's integrality is thus threatened
those held responsible for its continuity and for the structural form of its
continuity, the polity, in short, move to counteract the contagion of continuing breach, and endeavor first to contain, then dispel the crisis. These
agents of *redress* may be chiefs, elders, lawmen, judges, the military, priests,
shamans, diviners, fathers, mothers, Grand Juries, village pan-
chayats—often they are the repositories and representatives of legitimacy,
of conformity to established rules, standards, or principles.

   But it also happens that redressive agents and the instruments they have at command, courts, parliaments, assemblies, councils, armies, police, negotiating tables, divining apparatus, oracles, powers to curse or bless, have lost or are losing their authority, legitimacy, or efficacy in the eyes of the group members. The response to crisis may now emerge from a group intent on altering or restructuring the social order in some decisive way, reformative to revolutionary. Such a clash between conserving and reforming parties may create a new crisis as the representatives of the *ancien* and *nouveau régime* confront one another. Redress may then take the form of civil war, insurgency, or revolution. Much depends upon the size and scale of the group and the degree to which its social and economic division of labor has advanced. Such factors determine what modes of redress are applied or devised. In state societies with hierarchical social structures, failure to resolve crisis at the local or regional levels may result in redressive action by the central political or judicial authorities operating through their courts and police. In the simpler, preliterate, stateless societies redressive machinery is often of two kinds, jural or ritual. Jural action may mean informal or formal arbitration by elders, the summoning of a chief's court with councillors and assessors, or recourse to blood vengeance or feud. What is of special interest to us here is *ritual* action. In many small-scale societies what we distinguish in Western cultural tradition as social, moral, and natural orders are regarded as a single order with visible and invisible components. The term *"supernatural,"* like *"nature"* itself, is a Western theological-philosophical concept. Thus, illness or bad luck in the community, whether personal or epidemic, may be conceived as resulting from the action of invisible ancestral spirits, offended by covert or overt malicious deeds (witchcraft or quarrelling) among community members descended from them. Or it may be attributed to the hidden malice of living witches or sorcerors. If outbreaks of illness or a series of untoward events (plagues, locust, hurricanes, famine, drought, unexpected raids by outsiders, absence of genre animals) coincide with breaches of rules and relationships *within* the community, and there appears to be no rational settlement of dispute in terms of customary law, recourse may be had to divination or oracles, procedures to detect the invisible causes of conflict and to prescribe the appropriate type of ritual to propitiate or exorcise the afflicting spirit or witch's familiar. Such rituals, which I called "rituals of affliction" in the Central African contest, are found in many societies, and often develop an elaborate symbolism. Sometimes they are associated with cosmogonic or cosmological myths which explain how death and diseases of various kinds came into the world of men and women. Ritual in such societies is seldom the rigid, obsessional behavior we think of as ritual after Freud. Rather it is an orchestration of symbolic actions and objects in all the sensory codes—visual, auditory, kinesthetic, olfactory, gustatory—full of music and dancing and with interludes of play and entertainment. It may involve painting, including body painting, sculpture, wood carving, instrumental and choral music, systematic medical treatment (patients are given herbal potions and baths, steam inhalation, and so on, as part of the ritual process), dramatic plotting (ritual officiants often enact the roles of gods, cultural heroes, ancestors, or demons as described in myths), festal cuisine (certain kinds of food and drink are reserved for rites dedicated to specific gods or spirits), preaching and homiletic (for rituals of these types allow a good deal of freedom for innovative verbal behavior, often regarded as messages from spirits through possessed mediums or shamans), psychological analysis (diviners seek to probe the hidden tensions and grudges in the community that are believed to be responsible for affliction), dance drama and choreography according to set rules, and many more aesthetic and cognitive modes that later come to be specialized out as para-ritual, quasi-secular, then fully secularized professions in more complex societies.

Not only rituals of affliction but even life-crisis rituals (birth, puberty, marriage, funerary, and so forth) and seasonal rituals (first-fruits, harvest, solar solstice, and the like) have reference to conflict. Whereas rituals of affliction are sometimes a direct response to misfortune regarded as a manifest symptom of hidden conflict, the other main types may be viewed as *prophylactic* against conflict, anticipating and averting it by vividly demonstrating the blessings of cooperation. In my book, *The Forest of Symbols*, I have shown, for example, how both the boys' circumcision ritual (*Mukanda*) and the girls' puberty ritual (*Nkang'a*) among the Ndembu people of Zambia dramatize the characteristic divisions and oppositions between men and women in this matrilineal society, divisions arising from custom itself, where group placement, inheritance and succession are acquired through the mother's side; while power and authority, village headship and chieftainship, are held by men and women who leave their mothers and siblings to reside in their husbands' villages after marriage. This structural conflict between female structural continuity and male contemporary authority is "the undying worm" of Ndembu culture, even through ritual, myth, and symbol proliferate to mask it, cloak it, deflect it, or explain it away.

Briefly, I am saying that the performative genres of complex, industrial societies, as well as many of their forensic and judicial institutions, the stage and the law court, have their deep roots in the enduring human social drama, particularly in its redressive phase, the drama that has its *direct* source in social structural conflict, but behind which perhaps is an endemic evolutionary restlessness; for we seem to be a species that becomes easily bored with even its most advantageous cultural adaptations. Dostoevsky's Underworld Man despised Utopia, prizing his freedom of will to choose that which was not perfect, was even definable as criminal or sinful. And did not Goethe say: "He who strives unceasingly is not beyond redeeming" of seemingly fallen Faust? From this perspective social dramas keep us alive, give us problems to solve, postpone ennui, guarantee at least the flow of our adrenalin, and provoke us into new, ingenious cultural formulations of our human condition and occasionally into attempts to ameliorate, even beautify it.

However, in the simpler, preindustrial societies the full sequence of stages, breach, crisis, redress, restoration of peace through reconciliation or mutual acceptance of schism, may often run its course, since redress, whether legal or ritual, depends upon wide, even general popular agreement about values and on meaning. In complex, plural, class-, race-, age-, and gender-divided societies stressing competition, change, individualism, inventiveness, and innovation, it is less probable that general consensus on a national or pansocietal scale can be obtained. Nevertheless, for the same reasons, it is highly probable that a multitude of models for social order, utopian or otherwise, and a multiplicity of religious, political, and philosophical systems for assigning meaning to the typical events of the epoch, will be generated and operate through a wide variety of rhetorics and other means of persuasion. And since the individual-in-general rather than the social *persona* (the bundle of statuses and roles comprising the "social personality"), is both the generator and ultimate audience of these narrated, dramatized, or otherwise aesthetically coded models—the final appellate court, so to speak—there is no surety that in any major crisis full agreement will be reached on the terms under which peace and order will eventually be restored. Hence the contemporary paradox that in a world that respects learning, literacy, argument, negotiation, persuasion, legality, many major social dramas are settled by armed force, "by cutting the Gordian knot," the quick, simple solution to problems of any complexity or more than average perplexity. That is why so many nations are now under military rule. Where dissensus reigns as to meaning, consensus may be replaced by force. Of course, the forceful seizers of power and settlers of issues then endeavor to socialize the young in terms of a single, simplified belief system which defines legitimacy in such a way that social dramas will once more have agreed-upon mechanisms of redress, heavily charged with secular ritual. In such societies, the genres of cultural performance that have largely replaced the rituals and jural processes of tribal and feudal societies, in the course of their complexification into industrialized, urbanized polities and international mercantile systems, often fall under heavy political attack. The industrialized modes of retribalization on the scale of nations with which we have become familiar this century, whether Left, Right, or Center in political ideology—the totalitarian or totalistic systems—are united in their opposition to diversity in thought and lifestyle, for diversity leads to the *slow* resolution of social dramas on whatever level or place they may show up in the social process or national map, and this deferment of crisis-resolution may lead to a critiquing of the basic premises of the polity itself. Retribalization, it may be argued, on the scale of huge industrialized polities is really in sharp dialectical contradiction to the *modern* mode of production whose diversity and constant response to new technology (for example, computers, miniaturization, robotization of industry, and the like) demand equal diversity in the sphere of *culture*, especially in those aspects of culture concerned with the redressal, direct or indirect, of the social dramas constantly erupting from the new relations of production and giving rise to new kinds of social conflicts. Paradoxically, retribalization, "one Law for the Lion and the Ox" as Blake might have put it (which "is oppression"), is being carried on under the aegis of evolution to "a higher stage" of society. Retribalization, whether defined as "fascist," "socialist," "communist," or any other mode of authoritarian or totalistic control, must seek to control crisis of all types not only by force but also by reritualization of the third phase of all social dramas, that of redress—hence elaborately ritualized trials of heretics and renegades, most recently the Gang of Four in China. Thus, as individual human inventiveness and collective traditions of technical know-how penetrate the economic infrastructure, a contradiction arises between manifold and diverse forces and means of production, and monolithic state structures whose control of the means of production stifles creativeness at the level of the forces and relations of production.

Ritual, unlike theatre, does not distinguish between audience and performers. Instead, there is a congregation whose leaders may be priests, party officials, or other religious or secular ritual specialists, but all share formally and substantially the same set of beliefs and accept the same system of practices, the same sets of rituals or liturgical actions. A congregation is there to affirm the theological or cosmological order, explicit or implicit, which all hold in common, to actualize it periodically for themselves and inculcate the basic tenets of that order into their younger members, often in a graded series of life-crisis rituals, passages from birth to death, through puberty, marriage, initiation into prestigious secret societies, measured progress through an educational system which involves cumulative indoctrination, and so on. Theatre—from the Greek *theasthai*, "to see, to view"—is rather different. Schechner ("From Ritual to Theater and Back" in *Essays on Performance Theory*, 1977: 79) has recently argued that: "Theater comes into existence when a *separation* occurs between audience and performers. The paradigmatic theatrical situation is a group of performers soliciting an audience who may or may not respond by attending. The audience is free to attend or stay away—and if they stay away it is the theater that suffers, not its would-be audience. In ritual, stay-away means rejecting the congregation—or being rejected by it, as in excommunication, ostracism, or exile." One might add, that it is not a mortal sin if one fails to attend a play by Ibsen, Chekhov, Brecht or Ionesco, but that it used to be a mortal sin if one failed to attend Sunday Mass—in this case, one wonders whether the Catholic Church now sees itself as approaching the mode of theatre, even as it calls ironically for greater congregrational participation from those who do attend. In totalitarian states, it came to be regarded as sin if one did not attend a local rally for nationally dominant political figures—the non-attender was virtually a dissident.

Now back to my original point that everyday life is intrinsically connected with acting and vice versa. It seems to me that tribalism and would-be retribalization both stress *the social structure* and with it, the roles, statuses, positions that are its hierarchal components (summing up to the structural *persona*) at the expense of what social thinkers, from Durkheim to Kenelm Burridge, have called "the individual." The "person," Burridge argues, "is content with things as they are, the individual posits an alternative set of moral discriminations" (*Someone, No one: An essay on Individuality,* 1979:4). "The individual" or the individual-in-general is a concept arising rather late in most complex human cultures. Burridge relates its earlier forms to what I have called, following van Gennep, the *liminal period,* in rites of passage from one social state and status to another, at birth, puberty, marriage, death, and so on. The liminal period is that time and space betwixt and between one context of meaning and action and another. It is when the initiand is neither what he has been nor is what he will be. Characteristic of this liminal period is the appearance of marked ambiguity and inconsistency of meaning, and the emergence of liminal demonic and monstrous figures who represent within themselves ambiguities and inconsistencies. As ambiguous figures, they mediate between alternative or opposing contexts, and thus are important in bringing about their transformation. In our society we might see the "Theater of the Absurd" of Ionesco, Arrabal, and Beckett, as "liminal," though I would prefer the term "limin*oid*," however gratingly neologistic, as being at once akin to and perhaps deriving from the liminal of tribal and feudal rituals, and different from the liminal as being more often the creation of individual than of collective inspiration and critical rather than furthering the purposes of the existing social order. The incipient individual, in preliterate societies, does emerge, but often in veiled or restricted form. Burridge makes some interesting speculation about this *proto-* or *ur-* individual. He regards what he calls "the self," not as a static entity, but as a movement, an oscillating energy between the structural persona and the potentially antistructural individual. This enables him to write (*ibid.*: pp. 146-147): "The liminal period becomes an introduction to, and test of, moral being. Generally reenacting the transformation from nature to culture, pubertal rites bring the components of being together and confront the cultural faculties with the oppositions and correspondences between animal, moral, and spiritual beings. To use another idiom, the initiand is asked to measure communitas and anti-structure—wherein human beings, stripped of their roles, statuses, memberships, and moralities, are in communion as human selves—against the demands of organization and structure.

"In this situation," he continues, "most initiands, responding to past pressures of kinfolk and conformists, yield to the more obvious and overt side of the ritual. Some, intuitively grasping that symbols and symbolic activities contain a *mysterium*—a latency, a promissory note, an invitation to realize that which lies behind the obvious and overt—may perceive and order a truth which, because they cannot withstand conformist pressures, they will hold in their hearts all the years of their lives. Others lose themselves in the chaos, unable to bring it into order. A few persevere and are led into areas which the overtness of the cultural symbols hide from most. But while the affirmation of a truth discovered calls a halt, one negation breeds another and discovery becomes a continuing journey. Truth's center seems to grow more distant with each successive launch from closing peripheries. Each arrival entails a further moral choice if it is to make a new point of departure, and each departure requires a further transformation of the self in relation to otherness." Man grows through antistructure, and conserves through structure. Elsewhere, and evidently thinking of Durkheim's post-Renaissance "individual-in-general," Burridge writes of the individual as "the moral critic who envisages another kind of social or moral order, the creative spark poised and ready to change tradition. Yet if some people are wholly individuals and others are persons, it is a matter of common observation that most people are in some respects and most frequently persons, while in other respects and at other times they can appear as individuals. And this apparent oscillation or movement between person and individual—whether in a particular instance the movement is one-way or a return is made—may be identified as '*individuality*'. Or, 'individuality' refers to the opportunity and capacity to move from person to individual and/or vice versa . . ." (*ibid.*: pp. 5-6).

Burridge presumably means that in a society already characterized by the possibility of making many choices, a biological individual can opt to be a persona *in extremis*, a "Southern Colonel," "a Madam," "a Great Actor," "a Northern Senator," "a dear old schoolmaster," "a motherly soul," even an "eccentric," or an individual who eschews identification with all available social personas.

Theatre, in Western liberal-capitalist society, is a liminoid process, set in the liminoid time of leisure between the role-playing times of "work." It is, in a way, "play" or "entertainment" (which means, etymologically, "held-in-between," that is, it is a liminal or liminoid phenomenon). Originally, I have supposed it is one of the abstractions from the original pansocietal "ritual" which was part of the "work" as well as the "play" of the whole society before the division of labor and specialization split that great ensemble or gestalt into special professions and vocations. Originally theatre was concerned, among other things, with resolving crises affecting everyone and assigning *meaning* to the apparently arbitrary and often cruel-seeming sequence of events following personal or social conflicts.

The simple point I am trying to make—and much research is needed to bring in the necessary back-up evidence—is that in the simpler preindustrial societies, acting a role and exemplifying a status was so much a part of everyday life that the ritual playing of a role, even if it was a different role from that played in mundane life, was of the same *kind* as one played as son, daughter, headman, shaman, mother, chief, or Queen-sister. The difference between ordinary and ritual (or extraordinary) life, was mainly a matter of framing and quantity, not of quality. In ritual, roles were separated from their embedment in the ongoing flow of social life and singled out for special attention, or else they were seen as points of entry and exit on a continuous process (boy-to-man, girl-to-woman, commoner-to-chief, villager-to-member-of-hunting-cult, ghost-to-ancestor, and so forth) with some interesting transitional symbolism, and the shadowy appearance of the lineaments of the antistructural "individual" at some places and times. But in these societies acting was mainly role-playing; the *persona* was the dominant criterion of individuality, of identity. Thus, the great *collective* which articulated *personae* in hierarchical or segmentary structures was the real protagonist, both in life and ritual.

Against this symmetry between everyday life and its liminal double, ritual, we find the asymmetry of "life" *vis-a-vis* "acting" in post-Renaissance, pre-totalitarian Western societies. But now we detect an interesting contrast, even a paradox. For Western theatre has often posited, like Western art generally, a contrast between everyday life, whether work or that part of non-work devoted to institutionalized concerns, membership of family, sports club, charity organizations, union locals, secret societies (Elks, Masons, Knights of Columbus, and so forth), and *truly* antistructural life (private religion, taking part in the arts as creator or spectator, and the like). The *persona* "works," the *individual* "plays"; the former is governed by economic necessity, the latter is "entertained"; the former is in the indicative mood of culture; the latter in the subjunctive or optative moods, the moods of feeling and desire, as opposed to those cognitive attitudes which stress rational choice, full (if reluctant) acceptance of cause-and-effect, repudiation of mystical participation or magical affinities, calculation of probable outcomes of action, and awareness of realistic limitation on action. But theatre, though it has abandoned its former ritual, claims to be a means of communication with invisible powers and ultimate reality, and can still assert, particularly since the rise of depth psychology, that it represents the reality behind the role-playing masks, that even its masks, so to speak, are "negations of the negation." They present the false face in order to portray the possibility of a true face. Great theatre even brings incest and parricide on stage from behind the masks of kinship.

Theatre has, in fact, become the domain of the individual-in-general, of what post-Renaissance man and woman would call "the real self," or William Blake "the Individual" with his/her "Definite and Determinate

Identity." In modern theatre stage-roles undermined, in fact, everyday-life roles, declaring the latter "inauthentic." From this viewpoint, it is the *mundane* world that is false, illusory, the home of the *persona*, and theatre that is real, the world of the *individual*, and by its very existence representing a standing critique of the hypocrisy of all social structure which shape human beings, often by psychical and even physical mutilation (foot-binding, corsets, indigestible foods), in the image of abstract social status-roles. Of course, theatre, like *all* cultural forms, once it has become a recognized genre of performance, can be manipulated to support *both* conformative and subversive social and political positions. I am merely arguing that the rise of modern and postmodern theatre contains within it the seeds of a fundamental critique of *all* social structures hitherto known. The locus of *action*, such a view would hold, has shifted from "real life" in the "indicative mood" arenas of economics and politics to what has been hitherto held to be the world of play, fantasy, illusion, entertainment, known as theatre. This has been especially the case as religious ritual has been stripped of its flexible, ludic components, its sacred clowns, masked tricksters, riddling narratives, to make way for rigorous solemnity, serious and official discourse about privileged or transcendental "meanings" or "signifieds," to use the terminology of Saussure. Subjunctive "acting" is now what is "real," "authentic"; indicative "acting," in the so-called "real world" is seen as "hypocritical," "inauthentic," "bourgeois," "debasing"—though of late things social seem to be taking a reverse turn.

Some modes of "experimental theatre" have recently addressed themselves to the problem of presenting the whole role-playing world of mundane modern society with "acting" as its creative alternative, the stage as the locus of the emergent individual, alienated from himself in a world which insists on men and women masking themselves in a flickering series of shadowy personae. These are not the grand personae of tribal or feudal cultures, where the creation of oneself as a "public man" or "public woman" was a work of art, involving high style in dress, manners, and deeds as Richard Sennet demonstrates, but the picayune personae of office, factory, or classroom underlings, with only vestiges of familial personae left to manipulate at home for the dregs of a weary day. Here mundane, indicative-mood acting seems to be the domain of the fictive, the false, the rejection of "definite and determinate identity." It is against this "acting" that such masters of experimental theatre (who see theatre as the counterstroke which annihilates falsehood even when it "puts on plays") as Grotowski, Brook, Schechner, Suzuki, and others, with some ancestry in Stanislawski, Delsarte, Meyerhold, and even Artaud, have "re-acted" or "counter-acted." Take, for example, some recent notions of Grotowski (*On the Road to Active Culture: The Activities of Grotowski's Theater Laboratory Institute in the Years 1970-1977*, 1978:95-97). He is giving an interview to *Trybuna Ludu*:

Action in the sphere of active culture, such as gives one the feeling of fulfilling one's life, widening its scope, happens to be the need of many, but remains the domain of very few. Active culture is cultivated, for instance, by a writer when writing a book. We cultivated it while we were preparing performances. Passive culture—which is important and rich in aspects not easy to talk about right here—is a relationship to what is a product of active culture, that is to say, reading, watching a performance, film, listening to music. In certain, let us say, laboratory dimensions, we are working on means to *extend* the sphere of active culture. What is the privilege of the few, can also become the property of others. I am not talking about a mass production of works of art, but of a kind of personal creative experience, which is not indifferent for the life of an individual person, or his life with others. [Grotowski then states explicitly the view that acting is being, not performance.]

Working in the sphere of theater, preparing productions for many years, step by step we were approaching such a concept of active man/actor, where the point was not to act someone else, but to be oneself, to be with someone, to be in relationship, as Stanislawski used to call it.

In the past few years Grotowski seems to have abandoned theatre altogether to set out on what he calls "culture searches" or "paratheatrical experiments" like the 1977 (Summer) pilgrimage to Fire Mountain near Wroclaw in Poland, and the Global Village, a "kind of university of research," dispersed among many countries, "creative centers working alongside of various research and cultural centers in those countries" (*ibid.*: p. 103). The distinctive feature of those projects was the disappearance of the audience, and the development of ritualized experiences which, to my anthropologist's eye, bear a striking resemblance to the instructions and hazards typical of successive phases of boys' and girls' puberty rites in Central Africa. Here are some of the names of these "experiments" in both small and large groups, which may suggest anthropological comparisons to some readers: "Night Vigil," "The Way," "The Area of Fear," "The Circle of Rhythm," "The Circle of Darkness and Voice," "The Cutting" (*not*, we are relieved to learn, an exact parallel to the operation of circumcision, but a "violent though precise" dance. "Cutting" represents a vegetable cutting, "a seed of Meeting," that is a direct encounter between persons).

I use the word "persons" advisedly, for it seems to me that Grotowski, who is very much *persona grata* with the Polish Communist party, has abandoned the theatrical tradition in order to create new forms of ritual initiation which inscribe desirable personae on human prima materia, that is, form men and women in a humanistic image which is to replace older forms, especially those carried in the great religious traditions. The Western tradition of theatre kept the audience well in mind and respected its independent existence as the jury which decided on the rights and wrongs of the case presented by the dramatist, director, and actors. Here I would repeat what I wrote in a recent article called "Frame, Flow, and Reflection: Ritual and Drama in Public Liminality" (in M. Benamou and C. Caramello, *Performance in Postmodern Culture*, 1977:54): "I relish the separation of an audience from performers and the liberation of scripts from cosmology, ideology, and theology. The concept of individuality has been hard-won, and to surrender it to a new totalizing process of reliminalization is a dejecting thought." [I had distinguished "liminal" from "liminoid," by associating the first with obligatory, tribal participation in ritual and the second as characterizing artistic or religious forms voluntarily produced, usually with recognition of individual authorship, and often subversive in intention towards the prevailing structures.] "As a member of an audience I can see the theme and message of play as one among a number of 'subjunctive' possibilities, a variant model for thought or action to be accepted or rejected after careful consideration." [It may be that by paying for a ticket we have "bought" the author's and theatre's production as a "commodity," but we have not thereby been forced to "buy" his ideas or vision of reality.] "Even as audience people can be 'moved' by plays; they need not be 'carried away' by them—into another person's utopia or 'secular sacrum,' to use Grotowski's phrase. Liminoid theatre should limit itself to presenting alternatives: it should not be a brainwashing technique." To complete the sentence of William Blake I half-quoted earlier: "One Law for the Lion and the Ox is Oppression."

It is true that one of the aims of the Night Vigil at Grotowski's Laboratory Theater was to enable people to meet "out of their roles." But when one reads accounts of the way the "guides" of the Night Vigil "shepherd" persons towards the undertaking of certain physical acts (dancing, touching) or attaining certain psychological states, in such a way—to cite a psychologist disciple, Janina Dowlasz (*op. cit.*: p. 115)—"that healthy human emotions could release themselves again," one is uneasily reminded not only of circumcision rites in Central Africa but also of "Triumph of the Will." The role-stripped self is to be remolded by what Grotowski calls "the guides" into . . . what?

Here I would like to return to Burridge's argument for a moment before returning to postmodern theatre. After making the distinction between person and individual, he went on to consider individuality—which is the "apparent oscillation or movement between person and individual (for most people are both), whether in a particular instance the movement is one-way or a return is made. Or individuality may refer to the opportunity and capacity to move from person to individual and/or *vice versa* (*op. cit.*, pp. 5-6). I have tended to regard the social dimension of the individual as communitas, essentially a liminoid, voluntaristic mode of relating, a choosing of one another by total, integral human beings with limpidity of consciousness and feeling resulting, and sometimes the spontaneous generation of new ways of seeing or being. The social dimension of the person of *persona* is the activated social structure, the public domain of norm- or custom-governed relationships. But of course, nothing is so simple as that. Even Augustine had to admit that in real history the City of God and the Earthly City were hopelessly intermingled, and that compromises had continually to be made by the would-be denizens of the Urbs Coelestis if family life and urban politics were to be at all workable. Individuality seems to be something that has to be won—and one aspect of its winning, Burridge would say, is "an appreciation of own being in relation to traditional or alternative categories" (*op. cit.*: p. 6). Burridge sees initiation rites as compressed means of posing the person-individual dilemma, especially in their liminal periods, in terms of the given culture's experience and reflection of itself.

My own view is that the experimentalism of Schechner is directed toward the realization, through theatre, of individuality—somewhat in Burridge's sense—rather than toward the making of a new classless or "unalienated" man, in the zealot Grotowski manner. Schechner sees himself, in Kierkegaardian language, as a "midwife" rather than a Pygmalion. There was a time, he records, when he did try to mold the actors of his Performance Group in directions he considered "personally liberating." But there grew a rebellion in the ranks, and Schechner came to realize that he had become somewhat of a dictator, at any rate more than a director. Both Grotowski and Schechner—and indeed all directors in postmodern experimental theatre—advocate the supreme importance of "the rehearsal process," which involves very much more than the effectual realization of a playscript and the learning of parts. It involves innumerable workshop sessions, some lasting for hours, others all night, in which breathing exercises, voice workshops, ingenious games, psycho-dramas, dancing, aspects of yoga, and in Grotowski's "paratheater" at least, jumping in mudholes in the woods, represent components. All these disciplines and ordeals are aimed at generating communitas or something like it in the group. André Gregory, who ran a workshop in Wroclaw, (*On the Road to Active Culture*, 1978:42) stressed that this process also "means reaching to the inner recesses of the actor and back into his past. . .an attempt to reach him—as a human being—in his undersoil and roots . . . It is not important whether one creates art, which one gives to people, but it is important that men—-beings not indifferent to one another in life and in work—are included in the creative process . . . I needed Grotowski's theater not as someone connected with theater, or even as a spectator—I needed it as a human being."

Again I would emphasize: the language favored by Grotowski has moved away from that of performing a play to that of self-discovery and unmediated contact with and understanding of others. The rhetoric is religious, even though for Grotowski's disciples traditional religion is rejected. One is reminded of Durkheim's search for "secular substitutes" for both religion and ritual, and De Coubertin's conviction that he had found these in international athletics—a conviction leading to his successful establishment of the Olympic Games, a Hellenistic, humanistic, post-religious, international, highly ritualized festival celebrating what all humans have in common: a body capable of being disciplined (a kind of profane ascesis) and an agonistic drive (though this Darwinian competitiveness proved to be mainly a feature of Western culture).

One can see the attraction, the lure, of Grotowski's agenda. Let us create a liminal space-time "pod" or pilgrimage center, he seems to be saying, where human beings may be disciplined and discipline themselves to strip off the false personae stifling the individual within. There must clearly be a great sense of relief or release when the man and woman within emerge and are recognized. The idea of a return to nature is clearly connected with this emergence. But it is the experience of anthropologists that there are grave dangers in the initiatory processes. The initiand is usually being initiated *into* something; he or she may be released from one set of status-roles but only in order to be more firmly imprinted with another. The elders, the gurus, the masters of the circumcision lodge, the "guides," are there to make indelible marks (not merely in the form of bodily mutilation, circumcision, subincision, tooth-removal, scarification, and so forth, but also in the very psyche itself) on the generic human "prima materia" to which the initiands have been more or less willingly reduced. The subjective dimension of initiation, of all types of passage ritual, indeed, has not been given sufficient attention by anthropological investigators. We can learn a good deal from experimental theatre here. But one can see how a totalistic or totalitarian polity or regime might find the sophisticated elaboration of new secularized rites of passage, guided by certificated ideologists who understand the ritual process, very much to its taste.

To his credit Schechner has never forgotten that theatre is theatre and that entertainment is a fundamental part of it. Entertainment is liminoid rather than liminal, it is suffused with freedom. It involves profoundly the power of *play*, and play democratizes. Prospero realized this when he threw away his rod at the end of *The Tempest*. Schechner, though he has often been chided for taking liberties with an author's playscript, has never thrown out such a script completely. Rather he regards the script as a vital component in the rehearsal process, though he does not treat it as sacrosanct. It is an essential preliminary frame, to say the least, through which the rehearsal process must flow, though the extent and character of this frame may itself be modified, sometimes quite drastically, by the inner logic of that process. Other components have almost equal weight: the director, the actor, the environment, that is, the stage setting which is created anew for every production. All these, *and* the playscript, grow together, interact together, as the rehearsal process matures. Schechner is fond of quoting the child psychologist Winnecott's formulaton, "from *me* to *not-me* to *not-not-me*," to express this process to theatrical maturation. The *me*, the biological-historical individual, the actor, encounters the role given in the script, the *not-me*; in the crucible of the rehearsal process a strange fusion or synthesis of *me* and *not-me* occurs. Aspects of the actor's experience surface which tincture the script-role he or she has undertaken, while aspects of the dramatist's world-view or message embodied in the script and particularly as understood from the perspective of the "character" being played penetrate the essence of the actor as a human being. The director's role is mainly catalytic, he assists the alchemic or mystical marriage going on as the actor crosses the limen from *not-me* to *not-not-me*. The *me* at this third stage is a richer, if not deeper (I am unhappy about metaphors of "depth" here for they often rest on unconscious Western religio-philosophical assumptions) *me* than the *me* of the beginning.

But I am not here to attempt an exposition of Schechner's rehearsal techniques—he can obviously do this much better than I can. What I am saying, though, is that by keeping in hand the life-line of the playscript, the saving fiction, as it were, Schechner saves his theatre from what Jacques Derrida has called "the monological arrogance of 'official' systems of signification." And by keeping open the possibility of modifying the playscript—which, in a sense, also becomes a *not-me* and a *not-not-me*, like the actors themselves, the script itself may be saved from "the monological arrogance of official" interpretations which have tended to ossify poetic inspiration into "classical modes of presentation." Works of dramatic genius require many ages to be adequately, let alone fully, manifested; it is the task of each theatrical generation to rotate them anew in terms of its own experience. We are back with the loops of the horizontal figure eight again, the relationships of opposition and synthesis between social drama and aesthetic drama.

Entertainment! That's a key word. Literally, it means "to hold between," from OF *entre* between, and *tenir*, to hold. That is, it can be construed as the making of liminality, the betwixt and between state. Webster gives it both playful and serious valences, for it can mean (1) "to keep the interest of and give pleasure to; to divert; amuse," or (2) "to allow oneself to think about; have in mind; consider." Thus, in confession when the penitent told the priest that he had had lustful thoughts, the latter asked him, "But, son, did you entertain them?" His answer, honest enough, came quickly, "No, Father, but they entertained me." This ambiguity is the soul of theatre, which is not a mechanism of repression or even of sublimation, but fantasized reality even while it realizes fantasy. It also allows the spectator his human dignity, his right to treat all he sees in an as-if, subjunctive way. Schechner has recently tried to move to a general theory of performance as "a binary," one term of which is "efficacy-ritual" (with transformative intention, "changing" the participant), the other being "entertainment-theater." In my nomenclature these would represent a contrast between "liminal" and "liminoid" modes of performance. In actuality, they interpenetrate, though Grotowski would have the former prevail, and much of Broadway the latter. "Performance," writes Schechner (*Ritual, Play and Performance*, 1977: 218), "comprehends the impulse to be serious and to entertain; to collect meanings and to pass the time; to display symbolic behavior that actualizes 'there and then' and to exist only 'here and now'; to be oneself and to play at being others; to be in a trance and to be conscious; to get results and to fool around; to focus the action on and for a select group sharing a hermetic language, and to broadcast to the largest possible audiences of strangers who buy a ticket."

Back then, in the end, to our title whose ironies have been by no means dispelled by our peregrinations. When we act in everyday life we do not merely re-act to indicative stimuli, we act in frames we have wrested from the genres of cultural performance. And when we act on the stage, whatever our stage may be, we must now in this reflexive age of psychoanalysis and semiotics as never before, bring into the symbolic or fictitious world the urgent problems of our reality. We have to go into the subjunctive world of monsters, demons, and clowns, of cruelty and poetry, in order to make sense of our daily lives, earning our daily bread. And when we enter whatever theatre our lives allow us, we have already learned how strange and many-layered everyday life is, how extraordinary the ordinary. We then no longer need in Auden's terms the "endless safety" of ideologies but prize the "needless risk" of acting and interacting.

References

Boulton, Marjorie. *The Anatomy of Drama.* London: Routledge and Kegan Paul, 1971.

Burridge, Kenelm. *Someone, No One: An Essay on Individuality.* Princeton University Press, 1979.

Dowlasz, Janina. "Psychologist at Grotowski's," *Zicie Literackie,* No. 381538, pp. 111-115, September 18, 1977.

Geertz, Clifford. "Blurred Genres: The Refiguration of Social Thought." *American Scholar,* pp. 165-179, Spring, 1980.

Gregory, Andre. *On the Road to Active Culture.* Wroclaw: Grotowski Theatre Institute, 1978.

Hartnoll, Phyllis. *The Concise History of Theater.* New York: Harry N. Abrams, n.d.

Schechner, Richard. *Ritual, Play and Performance.* New York: The Seabury Press, 1977.

—. "Performers and Spectators Transported and Transformed," *Kenyon Review,* vol. III, no. 4, pp. 83-113, 1981.

Thomas, David Emil. "Mirror Images," *Scientific American,* vol. 2/3, no. 6, pp. 206-228, 1980.

Turner, Victor. "Frame, Flow and Reflection." In *Performance in Postmodern Culture,* M. Benamou and C. Caramello, eds. Madison, Wisconsin: Coda Press, 1977.

Index